Praise for *Propeller*

"The principles laid out in *Propeller* have helped us transform our company into a world-class organization. Adopting the book's practical method, focus on key results, and emphasis on creating a Culture of Accountability will improve any company's business outcomes."
—Scott Boatwright, chief restaurant officer, Chipotle

"*Propeller* builds on the foundation set with *The Oz Principle*, giving us continued excellent direction and insight to the most important but often neglected identifier of success within an organization . . . accountability. A term that is often used but rarely applied correctly and consistently. Read and reread *Propeller*!"
—Dale Murphy, retired Major League Baseball player, two-time National League MVP, Atlanta Braves

"The concepts in *Propeller* have changed the way I view my business and my life. It has made a positive impact on my interactions, both personal and professional. By keeping myself accountable, I can role model what accountability looks like, improving my relationships."
—Susan Carroll, president, Inova Fairfax Medical Campus

"This book reveals the power of personal accountability and how you can use the simple tools and techniques described to empower your organization to achieve results you thought were out of reach"
—Robert Anderson, president, OSF HealthCare Saint Francis Medical Center

"No matter what challenge your business is facing, *Propeller* is one of the most powerful ways to drive results by fully engaging and leveraging your entire organization."
—Elaine J. Thibodeau, platform leader, Johnson & Johnson Surgical Vision

"Simply put, this approach *works*. The tools and techniques give a team—any team in any type of organization—a framework that is clear, understood at all levels, and enables each individual within the organization to take responsibility for his or her role and contributions. It is powerful, effective, and clear—and it works! Honest."

—Elaine Ullian, retired CEO, Boston Medical Center

"The principles in *Propeller* gave us tools we didn't know we needed until we had them. Now our organization is actively building a culture of accountability that delivers results—and perfectly complements our mission to serve with the greatest care and love."

—Sister Diane Marie McGrew, president, OSF HealthCare

"Many leaders struggle with influencing their organization's culture. They sometimes even have the opposite impact from the results that they intended because they overcomplicate things and end up providing negative experiences for their employees. The brilliance of the approach to getting results that is articulated in *Propeller* is its elegant simplicity. In working with Partners In Leadership over the years, I haven't seen anything that even comes close. Leaders adopt the techniques and strategies quickly, using a common language and practical tool set that become deeply embedded in the way that the company operates."

—Kevin Munson,
head of Leadership Development, Dish Network

Propeller

Propeller

Accelerating Change by
Getting Accountability Right

TANNER CORBRIDGE, JARED JONES,
CRAIG HICKMAN, AND TOM SMITH

PORTFOLIO/PENGUIN

Portfolio/Penguin
An imprint of Penguin Random House LLC
penguinrandomhouse.com

Most Portfolio books are available at a discount when purchased in quantity
for sales promotions or corporate use. Special editions, which include person-
alized covers, excerpts, and corporate imprints, can be created when purchased in large quantities. For more information, please call (212) 572–2232 or
email specialmarkets@penguinrandomhouse.com. Your local bookstore can
also assist with discounted bulk purchases using the Penguin Random House
corporate Business-to-Business program. For assistance in locating a participating retailer, e-mail B2B@penguinrandomhouse.com.

ISBN: 9780525537830 (hardcover)
ISBN: 9780525541271 (ebook)

Printed in the United States of America

10   9   8   7   6   5   4   3   2   1

Contents

Propeller

Introduction

THE POWER OF GETTING ACCOUNTABILITY RIGHT

Only when you assume full accountability for your thoughts, feelings, actions, and results can you direct your own destiny, otherwise someone or something else will. That's *The Oz Principle,* plain and simple. For the past twenty-five years, organizations around the world have implemented this principle as a *Propeller* to accelerate change by getting accountability right, C-suite to front line.

Throughout our careers, we have worked with thousands of leaders who decidedly advanced their careers, teams, and companies by infusing a positive brand of personal accountability into their organizations. These are leaders who reject the face-saving cover of excuses and denial and choose instead to own their circumstances and their results—leaders who purposefully and persistently ascend the Steps to Accountability in relentless pursuit of game-changing performance.

Naturally, all businesses, teams, and leaders flounder at times for many reasons. Sometimes they get off track by pursuing a faulty strategy, other times by making a poor organizational decision or failing to execute on market adjustments quickly enough. The list of reasons goes on and on. However, the secret to learning and correcting quickly lies in how the leader, team, and company evaluate such challenging failures. If a blame-oriented or consequence-focused approach to accountability is applied, learning, correction, and growth suffer enormously. That's how leaders get accountability wrong. In the pages that follow, we will illustrate with great clarity how getting accountability wrong comes with a very high price.

Ask any CEO or senior leader, and most will readily acknowledge the mistakes they've made. The most influential leaders, however, demonstrate a unique ability to make egoless adjustments to their previous decisions. They take total ownership for current circumstances and inspire a sense of optimism within the teams they lead. These are the leaders who get accountability right. And when they do, everyone who works with them wins. Regardless of the need—regaining lost stability or building on success—the formula applied by these leaders for accelerating change is the same: With intentionality, resolve, and vision, they define the results they need to achieve and then inspire people to rise above their circumstances and demonstrate the ownership needed to perform at new heights. They get accountability right and use it to propel their people and teams forward.

Of course, even the strongest among us will slip into victimhood from time to time. Nobody's perfect. Everyone, even the highest achievers in our complex interconnected society, can get stuck in the blame game or victim cycle on occasion, but those who take accountability for results and are successful in achieving them never remain in that cycle for long. Take CEO Steve Fisher, for example. When Steve moved from CFO to CEO of Novelis, the world's largest producer of flat-rolled aluminum, he knew full well that the company's future depended on quick and decisive action. Having worked for the company as CFO for several years, he had witnessed firsthand the challenges and opportunities that had to be tackled head-on. Upon becoming CEO, Steve didn't waste any time acting on what he knew needed to happen. At a pivotal Global Leadership Team meeting he decided to take the first step.

On day one of the meeting, the team anxiously waited to enter the Ritz-Carlton ballroom for the company's annual Global Leadership Summit. They could smell the aroma of freshly brewed coffee wafting from the large silver urns in the lobby. While they took comfort from the familiar surroundings, they suspected this would not be the same old annual meeting. Everyone looked expectantly at their new CEO leaning against a wall near the ballroom doors. Although Steve had dressed down for the occasion, wearing jeans and a button-down long-sleeve shirt, he exuded a quiet, yet intense confidence they had not seen before. Although Steve did not see himself as exceptional in any particular way, those who knew him well regarded him as "smart and gifted." What made him even better was his ability to interact with others and create an environment of trust. He was approachable, treated people with courtesy and respect, and took time to reach out to those who worked the floor at their factories. The Global Leadership Team had gotten to know him over the years, and they liked what they saw. One senior executive said that in spite of his talent, "There's no ego with Steve."

Steve had attended his share of these Novelis Global Leadership summits. The annual gathering of the company's top two hundred leaders convened every mid-March at the Ritz-Carlton on the outskirts of Atlanta, Georgia. During his eight-year tenure as CFO, he had enjoyed rubbing shoulders with the company's senior leaders from Brazil, Germany, Korea, and a dozen other countries. The positive reputation he had created over his time as CFO only heightened the palpable anticipation felt throughout the room for what lay ahead.

For the past few years Novelis had been posting dismal financial performance, pursuing conflicting priorities, tarnishing its reputation with customers, perpetuating stubbornly uncommunicative organizational silos, and suffering from a lack of ownership and accountability for results. Everyone felt it, from the two hundred leaders attending this meeting to the company's eleven thousand employees around the world. And to top it off, despite several years of unprecedented investment totaling more than $2 billion, Novelis had not shown an ability to produce a favorable return on invested capital. The company was continuing along the same old course, like a runaway yacht racing toward a rocky shore. The question on everyone's mind was, "What's it going to take to turn Novelis around?"

As the Global Leadership Team funneled into the ballroom, Steve found a quiet corner to collect his thoughts. Convincing this group of diverse people from around the globe that Novelis needed to take bold steps to deal with the company's declining financial performance would take every ounce of his energy and skill. Every word from his mouth had to be credible, clear, and compelling. As the music began to fade, the lights dimmed, and something like the voice of God announced, "Welcome to Novelis's Global Leadership

Summit. Please welcome to the stage your CEO, Steve Fisher." The audience applauded enthusiastically.

Steve strode onto the stage, stopped at the podium, and waited for the room to grow quiet. Then he spoke in a quiet tone. "You might not see it right now, but we have the opportunity to do something extraordinary. We have the chance to turn this company around, achieve a level of unprecedented results, and help some of the world's largest vehicle manufacturers achieve their results by reducing their emissions to levels never thought possible. There is a blue ocean of opportunity in front of us. However, as a company, I've become convinced we will drown in that ocean if the people in this room don't change. *Accountability* must be our vehicle for change."

Accelerating change by getting accountability right, C-suite (CEO, CFO, COO, CMO, CHRO, CTO, etc.) to front line became the company's primary propeller for growth. In just two years under Steve Fisher's leadership, the senior team at Novelis led and achieved an astonishing transformation by getting people to take greater accountability for their results. The change was not only dramatic but inspiring. Engagement scores rose to historic levels. Return on capital employed (ROCE) almost tripled, profitability increased 26 percent to $1.2 billion, and cash flow grew by 471 percent. The huge influx of cash helped fund a big acquisition and expanded Novelis's presence into high-value markets such as aerospace. People, once mired in the blame game, began to take personal accountability for the results they were achieving and refused to blame others as they did so.

Novelis's historic transformation came about because a dedicated and savvy leader diligently applied the Steps to Accountability (See It, Own It, Solve It, Do It) throughout his organization. That brought the necessary focus, clarity, alignment, and accountability around the key results that Novelis needed to deliver. Eleven thousand people at Novelis discovered that they possessed all the talent and skill they required to deliver their results and turn the company's "crossroads moment" into a spectacular triumph.

You will meet a lot of leaders like Steve Fisher in this book, real people working in real organizations, who have benefited from the principles of taking accountability for results. Partners In Leadership has crafted and honed these principles over the past thirty years as it has helped thousands of organizations rely on the power of positive accountability to achieve the results they needed. Stories from Chili's Grill & Bar, Johnson & Johnson, Sutter Health, Lockheed Martin, Domino's, Boston Medical Center, Chipotle, and many other *Fortune* 1000 companies will make these principles come alive, so you can easily apply them in your own teams and organizations.

There is a powerful parallel between this book's predecessor, *The Oz Principle,* written in 1994 and revised in 2004, and L. Frank Baum's classic story *The Wonderful Wizard of Oz.* In the novel and the movie, Dorothy and her companions learn that no matter how difficult your circumstances, the power to address your challenges and achieve the results you desire lies inside you, not in some external force or in the hands of some guru pulling levers behind a velvet curtain. This book will help you implement *The Oz Principle* to propel your team and organization forward to new levels of performance.

We chose the title *Propeller* for this book because it captures in one word what *The Oz Principle* and the Steps to Accountability create: *accelerated movement in a needed direction.* No matter how daunting the obstacles you face, this book will deepen your resolve to take accountability for your results—past, present, and future. Such resolve moves leaders, teams, and organizations to choose optimism when pessimism is justified, to accept responsibility when blaming others is easily explained, and to move forward and win when giving up is understandable.

Certainly, a lack of accountability can creep into any team or organization. It may first come unannounced as a reasonable explanation for why we didn't deliver; then it may escalate into a more aggressive series of blame-oriented accusations pinpointing who's at fault; and inevitably, over time, it simply becomes "the way we do things around here." That sort of thinking always leads to failure. Success comes from taking accountability for better results. Make *that* "the way we do things around here." That's what Steve Fisher did at Novelis. That's what *Propeller* can do for you.

Chapter One

ACCOUNTABILITY FOR KEY RESULTS

Applying the Oz Principle, C-Suite to Front Line

Have you ever looked at the people around you—at work, in your circle of friends, or in your extended family—and wondered why some are succeeding and growing in their careers while others seem stagnant or frustrated by life? Why do some individuals achieve the results they want while others explain what went wrong along the way? Do you wonder the same thing as you look at the teams of people you work with? Why do some teams generate a powerful sense of unity and purpose in their work while other teams limp along divided in purpose, blaming one another for failing to deliver? We think the answer is accountability.

For years we have observed a pervasive problem in our society: a serious and growing lack of accountability inside corporations, institutions, governments, associations, and even families. None of us need to look beyond the daily news broadcasts to find the blame game being played out in dramatic detail. In our work, we are constantly interacting with leaders who are fed up with the blame game that has taken root in their day-to-day work environments. They are frustrated by and concerned about the amount of time and energy they waste listening to explanations and justifications from individuals, teams, or departments about why they aren't going to deliver the needed results when they should be discussing ideas and solutions for overcoming obstacles and setbacks. In many cases, people in organizations grow numb to the "blame game" as it metastasizes into a broadly accepted organizational narrative. Adding to the frustration, leaders also complain that nothing has changed from the previous year's annual employee engagement survey. All of the leaders we've interacted with over the years have had one thing in common: They knew the solution was to create greater ownership and accountability, but they didn't know how to do it in an effective and successful way. That's why *The Oz Principle* was published in the first place, it's why it was published again in a second edition in 2004, and it's why we're now publishing *Propeller*, with new insights and a unique focus on implementing the principles of the original groundbreaking classic.

In the upcoming pages, we'll explore the accountability paradox—*the more we hold people accountable the wrong way, the less accountability we actually get*—and show you how to resolve it quickly. We'll also introduce you to a few simple principles and models, honed and proven over thirty years of research, observation, and application in client organizations. As we mentioned in the introduction, the stories and examples we'll share with you have been chosen from literally thousands of client engagements.

What Does It Really Take to Get Accountability Right?

Consider what images spring to mind when you hear the word *accountability*. Most likely you picture some sort of punishment for a mistake, perhaps someone in authority holding your feet to the fire or hammering you for wrongdoing. We've spent decades combating and redefining that negative view of accountability because reinforcing accountability in a negative way only disenfranchises people and kills morale. In our view, accountability is not an accounting for misdeeds or a reckoning for one's missteps; it's a powerful motivator for getting results. Individuals, teams, and entire organizations that use a positive and engaging approach to accountability are able to propel themselves toward achieving the results they need. Moreover, we recommend that you never again think of accountability as something someone else does *to* you; it's something you do *for* yourself, your team, and your organization to help you grow and get better results.

In a superb illustration of individuals and teams taking accountability for their own results, we found ourselves standing on the tail section of a massive military aircraft, looking five stories down to the tarmac as we asked Ray Burick, one of the key leaders at Lockheed Martin, "Why do you need us here?"

Looking down at the plane, Ray said, "We're behind schedule and over budget. You see those guys working on the wing? They're doing their job and working really hard to do it right. You see those guys working on the fuselage, the main section of the plane where the wing connects? They're working super hard to get everything done that needs to be done. Now move up the fuselage and look at the cockpit and watch the team tackling that amazing bundle of wires feeding the control panel. They are doing everything they feel they are supposed to do to finish their section of the plane."

So, we asked, "What's the problem?"

Ray continued, "When the wing is handed off to the fuselage team, something inevitably needs to be tweaked or adjusted. So, the fuselage team blames the wing team for not doing its work thoroughly enough. They kick everything back to the wing team and wait for the corrections to be made. Meanwhile, the wing team blames the fuselage team for not following the plans properly and complains that it didn't do what it was asked to do and then blames the planning team for not being clear. While this is going on, the work on the plane comes to a halt until someone figures out what to do next. They're all focused on their own *sections* of the plane. I need you guys [Partners In Leadership] because I have to redefine what the job is. I don't need them to take accountability for the wing or cockpit; I need them to take accountability for the *entire* plane getting out the door on time and under budget."

This is a classic example of the myopic, departmental thinking that afflicts many organizations, large and small, across the globe. Moreover, it epitomizes what we call the blame game. And it's the blame game that both poisons the well of problem solving and diverts energy away from delivering the key results. "It's not my fault! Someone else screwed up!" or "I'm paying for *their* mistakes. Hold *them* accountable." Of course, finger-pointing and playing the victim will never help you move the needle closer to delivering the results you need, whether you're trying to implement continuous improvement initiatives, inspire innovation, improve customer experiences, retain top talent, or grow top and bottom lines. Achieving any of these results depends more than anything else on getting people to rise above their circumstances and constantly ask, "What else can I do to get the result?" Sadly, too many people pay lip service to accountability while clinging to the old, tired definition of meting out punishment for something that went wrong.

After a few months of intense focus, Ray Burick was successful in shifting the mind-set of his team at Lockheed Martin. He got them to see their jobs in terms of the results they needed to deliver together. And the impact was a complete turnaround. The team began to take accountability for something more than their piece of the finished product—they began taking accountability for delivering the whole plane. Their watch cry changed from doing their job to achieving the results—results they were accountable to deliver. Within nine months the team was not only back on schedule, they were now delivering better quality, doing it under budget, and beating their aggressive timelines.

To get accountability right, leaders must have a common understanding of what it is and how to speak clearly and consistently about its meaning. Stop and ask ten different people you work with what they think accountability means. More than likely you will hear ten different answers. Unfortunately, ten different answers will impede any organization from experiencing the propelling power of getting accountability right.

A number of years ago we began looking at how dictionaries define accountability. Most say something like the following:

Accountability: subject to having to report, explain, or justify; liable; responsible; answerable.

Let's consider the first two words used in the dictionary definition of accountability: "Subject to." Clearly, "subject to" suggests that accountability is something done to you and not something you choose for yourself. The next two words, "having to," further support this conclusion. Both "subject to" and "having to" constitute weak, non-propelling views of accountability. The words "explain" and "justify" direct us to come up with a good story when failing to deliver on expected outcomes. And in this context, "liable" and "responsible" urge simply falling on your sword and taking the blame when things go wrong or becoming "answerable" when results are not forthcoming. What an uninspiring and inaccurate definition of accountability.

This negative interpretation of accountability explains the discomfort people have when answering the question "Who's accountable?" Nobody wants to raise their hand in answer to that question given the common definition we see in use today. No wonder accountability is used as a hammer when people make mistakes or commit blunders. Sadly, it's an inherently flawed view of accountability—doomed from the first minute it's applied—that actually invites the sort of excuse making that can keep individuals, teams, and entire organizations from accelerating change and getting the results they need. We much prefer thinking of accountability as a tremendously positive force, not something someone else does to punish you, but something you do for yourself in order to get better results. It strikes us that dictionaries glaringly omit *results* from their description of accountability. From our experience, there's not another word associated with accountability that is more important than the word *results*. When defined correctly and commonly understood throughout an organization, accountability propels individuals and teams to think differently, collaborate better, and consistently demonstrate the ownership necessary to achieve the results they need to deliver.

Getting accountability right begins with a common understanding of what it is. When we talk about the propelling power of accountability, we are referring to the definition we first introduced in *The Oz Principle* and have since applied to accelerate the growth of millions of people in thousands of client organizations:

Accountability: a personal choice to rise above one's circumstances and demonstrate the ownership necessary for achieving desired results; to See It, Own It, Solve It, and Do It.

This definition suggests that accountability begins with a decision to do something to create a better outcome. It urges the person taking accountability to avoid the temptation of falling victim to difficult circumstances and embrace the opportunity of working toward a better end result. No one *gives* accountability to you; you must *take* it. When you take it, you put yourself in charge of the outcomes you want and need to deliver. Ask leaders in any organization how they got ahead in their careers, and you'll seldom hear any of them say, "I was held accountable by the people above me." You'll more likely hear something along the lines of "I made a decision early on that my future rested in my own hands and that only I could move myself forward by working effectively with others to deliver the needed results."

You have the power to get the results you want.

We have found that when you classify organizations according to their approach to accountability, they fall into one of two categories: (1) Accountability means explanation, justification, and punishment, or (2) accountability means taking charge of your role in getting results for yourself, your team, and your organization. In the first category of organizations, people think in terms of holding *others* accountable for what has happened; in the latter, people believe in holding *themselves* accountable for what happens next. Consider the stark differences:

A Culture of Explanation, Justification, and Punishment

- People fail to collaborate and constantly blame each other.
- People fail to take personal initiative and do not actively engage.
- People tend to duck and hide when they see a problem.
- People fear reprisal for speaking candidly or making the wrong decision.
- People avoid taking risks.

- People feel threatened by the talents and achievements of others.
- People feel like personal growth and career progress are being dictated by everyone else.

A Culture of Accountability for Results

- People constantly look at what else they can do and refuse to blame others when something goes wrong.
- People are engaged and freely offer ideas to make things better.
- People actively attack every problem they see.
- People seek, provide, and act on feedback.
- People learn from mistakes and failures.
- People are not threatened by the talents of others but leverage them appropriately to solve problems.

Which culture do you prefer? Whether you sit in the C-suite or work on the shop floor, playing the blame game will get you nowhere and it will eventually paralyze your personal growth. Only by taking accountability can you expect to achieve what matters most to you, your team, and your organization.

Accountability Principles

If you ask a hundred managers across a sampling of *Fortune* 1000 companies, "Do you see a need for greater accountability and ownership in your organization today?" 100 percent will likely say, "Absolutely!" If you follow up that question with another question,

"Are *you* personally accountable?" again, 100 percent will likely say, "Yes, of course!" Rarely will someone say, "I'm a train wreck. Don't count on me to deliver anything." This presents one of the ironies that surround the idea of accountability. Most people want to see more accountability, yet few recognize that they need to *take* more accountability. No raindrop ever feels responsible for the deluge, though each contributes to the flood. The same holds true in organizations, large and small. Each and every missed opportunity to take greater accountability contributes to shaping a culture of explanation, justification, and punishment.

Three basic principles will help you harness the power of accountability:

1. Understand the Steps to Accountability That Promote Ownership and Propel Change.
2. Apply the Model to Yourself to Reduce Time Spent Below the Line.
3. Adopt the Common Language of Accountability to Accelerate Movement.

Let's look closely at these three fundamental principles.

1. Understand the Steps to Accountability That Promote Ownership and Propel Change

This model, which can be captured at a glance, promotes greater accountability at all levels of the organization:

THE STEPS TO ACCOUNTABILITY

For most people, the first thing that jumps out at them as they look at the Steps to Accountability model is the line in the middle. That line separates the unproductive, time-wasting, results-impeding blame game from the Steps to Accountability that must be taken in order to deliver results. Below the Line, people focus on what they can't control, they play the victim, ignore and deny the problem, point their finger at others, cover their tails in order to get themselves off the hook, claim that it's not their job, act confused while expecting someone else to tell them what to do, or just wait to see if the issue or problem will magically resolve itself. Above the Line, people focus on what they can control and they assume account-ability for resolving issues or problems by taking four sure steps toward getting the right result: They See It, Own It, Solve It, and Do It. People who languish Below the Line prepare stories that explain why past efforts went awry; people who reside Above the Line empower themselves to strive for better results. Below the Line, people become fixated on what's happening to them. Above the Line, people focus on what they want to happen next. Below the Line, people use smoke and mirrors to delay and buy themselves more time. Above the Line, people demonstrate a sincere desire to deliver the right results. Below the Line, people think, "How else do I explain and justify why it's so hard to deliver?" Above the Line people ask themselves, "What else can I do to get results?"

While the model looks quite simple . . .

Don't let the model's simplicity fool you!

Hurricane Katrina ripped through New Orleans several years ago, devastating the area and changing the lives of thousands of people. Making matters worse, the government bungled its response to the catastrophe. When Congress summoned Michael Brown, the director of the Federal Emergency Management Agency (FEMA), to explain what had gone wrong, he offered a well-crafted story. Those who understand the Steps to Accountability will quickly recognize that Brown's testimony was pure justification for why what was happening was not his fault. For Brown, Hurricane Katrina brought with it a perfect storm for hiding from the truth. We call it the

Victim Cycle. As he spoke to Congress, Brown hit every Below the Line button:

- Ignore/Deny: "I had no idea how bad Louisiana's emergency preparation plans were."
- It's Not My Job: "We're FEMA, we're not the first responders. We provide support and bring resources to the problem."
- Finger-pointing: "If the first responders [local authorities] had evacuated the city when we told them to, this situation would have been much different."
- Confusion/Tell Me What to Do: "There is a lot going on down there, and we're working hard to prioritize and chip away at the problems."
- Cover Your Tail: "Have you seen how much time I've had to spend talking to the media? That's time that could have been used to work on the problem."
- Wait and See: "We have good people down there now, so you'll see things getting better soon."

Brown chose to go Below the Line and justify his response to Katrina. But people who understand the Steps to Accountability model are much more apt to work Above the Line, solving problems and making the necessary adjustments to get better results. Those who understand this model and apply it to themselves will reduce the time they spend Below the Line, improve their personal performance, and lead others to achieve the desired results.

2. Apply the Model to Yourself to Reduce Time Spent Below the Line

Take a moment to consider a significant problem you faced that made it difficult to achieve the result you needed to deliver. How did you explain it to others? When describing it to friends outside the company or to a family member, did you sound like Michael Brown as he justified his lack of progress to Congress? His Below the Line explanations touched on the truth, just as yours might: "Our competition's disruptive new product completely blindsided us." Brown was describing real problems that attended the aftermath of Hurricane Katrina, but each of his statements also implied that his agency was a victim of circumstances it could not overcome. We cite Michael Brown's testimony before Congress because of how thoroughly it demonstrates what Below the Line responses sound like. But you don't need to go back to Hurricane Katrina to see perfect examples of this mind-set.

Consider what's happening around you on a daily basis. There are probably plenty of people thinking and acting both Below the Line and Above the Line in your world. Are you currently Below the Line on an issue, problem, initiative, relationship, or key result? Where are you failing to deliver at the level you need to? How can you minimize the time you spend Below the Line and maximize the time you spend Above the Line to deliver on your commitments? If you apply the Steps to Accountability model to yourself and your work environment, you will recognize people languishing in Below the Line categories in one way or another. And wherever results are being achieved, you will find people working Above the Line, taking the Steps to Accountability. Write down your thoughts and observations. Don't forget to look at yourself and be honest.

We worked with the CEO of one of the largest grocery chains in the U.S., who had purchased a copy of *The Oz Principle* and decided to read it between store visits. As he started off around 9:00 a.m., he and his driver headed for his first store. Nobody knew he was coming to their store and he liked it that way. As he began reading he found himself intrigued with the Steps to Accountability model. He read about what it looks like to be Below the Line and just as he finished reading about Ignore/Deny, It's Not My Job, and Finger-pointing, he entered his first store of the day. He was surprised by how many supervisors were using one of these three Below the Line categories to explain why they were not achieving one of their key store metrics. Between the first and second store visits, he continued reading about Confusion/Tell Me What to Do, Cover Your Tail, and Wait and See. When he arrived at the second store, he was surprised to hear the same kinds of excuses. The store manager actually used the very words "I'm confused. Why don't you just tell me exactly what you want me to do and I'll go do it." It was then, only two stores into his day, that he realized he was part of the problem. He had become way too comfortable with telling his people exactly what to do. Suddenly, he realized that as he told people exactly what to do and they did it, he was the only one taking accountability for what needed to be done in the stores.

By the end of the day he knew that he had an organization full of Below the Line leaders. In fact, he learned that some of his store managers were already creating their explanations for why they were going to miss this year's store budgets. He couldn't believe it—they were only six months into their year and these managers were ready to raise the white flag in surrender. What's worse, many of his managers and supervisors seemed to believe that if they could explain and justify their poor performance, they would take themselves off the hook for failing to achieve the agreed-upon store metrics.

We learned about the CEO's realization early the next morning when the company's VP of human resources called to ask about our availability for a meeting. Shortly thereafter, we were working with that CEO to create a Culture of Accountability throughout this vast chain of grocery stores. It didn't take long for the grocery store chain to start growing again. Store sales increased year after year for the next several years. That's the propelling power of *The Oz Principle.*

As you apply this model to yourself please keep in mind that bad things *do* happen to people and businesses and most likely will happen again. You are not accountable for everything that happens to you. People have lost homes to natural disasters. Companies have been blindsided by innovative disruption. But your willingness and courage to move forward in a positive direction, despite the trials, are the keys to getting accountability right.

Only by moving Above the Line and taking each of the Steps to Accountability can people overcome obstacles and achieve the results they want. When people get stuck Below the Line complaining about the vicissitudes of life and the tough realities of business, they become too slow to rebuild homes and cities, and too late to create needed innovations to leapfrog or even respond to their disruptive competitors.

Having said that, there's not one of us who is immune to giving in to the temptation to take ourselves off the hook with one excuse or another:

- "I didn't have enough time."
- "That's not my job."
- "The schedule is too tight."
- "We need more resources."
- "It's the boss's fault."
- "I didn't know."
- "The whole economy is in the tank."
- "Things will get better tomorrow."
- "The competition outsmarted us."
- "Our marketing department is broken."

Whatever the wording, all of our justifications for failure proclaim, "Why I can't do it," rather than "What else can I do?" In far too many organizations, Below the Line has become the norm rather than the exception. Imagine how much more you could accomplish if, rather than sitting around feeling sorry for yourself or waiting for your circumstances to magically improve, you climbed Above the Line and took accountability for improving your situation. If an organization has ten thousand employees and they all spend just one day per week Below the Line, then as a whole the people in that organization are spending four million hours per year trapped Below the Line, where nothing grows, gets better, or is achieved. Imagine what else might happen if that same company was able to invest an additional four million hours of talent in seeking and finding solutions.

It's not wrong to go Below the Line. It's human nature. We all let the gravitational force that accompanies victim thinking pull us Below the Line into the realm of excuse making when things go wrong or challenges confront us. But all of us can acknowledge that it's totally ineffective to stay there, continually rationalizing and explaining why we're stuck and can't move forward. When we find ourselves Below the Line, the best thing we can do is acknowledge where we are and choose to move Above the Line. The best question we can ask when we recognize we're Below the Line is "What else can I do to achieve the result?" That single question will lift each of us Above the Line and motivate us to See It, Own It, Solve It, and Do It.

3. Adopt the Common Language of Accountability to Accelerate Movement

The Above the Line and Below the Line language is sticky because of its simplicity and intuitiveness. Whenever we revisit a company after having taught people how to use the Steps to Accountability model, we always find them using the model's language to talk about their work. Above the Line, the Line, and Below the Line become an integral part of their daily discussions as they seek to solve problems and move forward. Adopting common performance management language gets everybody on the same page. To further embed the common language into their cultures, many of our clients display graphics of the model in offices and conference rooms. Some go beyond that. The leaders of one of our client's large manufacturing plants wanted the Above the Line message to be the first thing their people saw when they arrived at work, so they stretched a massive banner across the back wall of the plant facility. It read: The Air Is Better Above the Line!

In another example, we were meeting with one of Europe's largest medical products manufacturers in an old German convent barn that had been converted into a corporate conference center. While working with the executive team to clarify its key results, the CEO told us he was about to confront a perplexing issue. So, we anticipated that the upcoming meeting might get a bit uncomfortable. As the meeting began, the CEO explained that the organization was at significant risk of missing its annual profit target for the first time in several years. His usually calm voice rose as he said, "We have only nine weeks left in our financial year, and I have not seen the level of concern and urgency I know this situation requires."

The CEO had confided earlier, in a moment of candid frustration, that the blame game was sucking up considerable energy from his team. Finance was blaming the managing directors of the various global regions for not hitting their revenue targets. The managing directors were blaming manufacturing for not delivering their best-selling surgical products on time, the country managers were blaming new-product development for not producing new products quickly enough, and new product development was blaming manufacturing for not prioritizing production of the new products they had developed. Meanwhile, manufacturing, which was already producing over fifty-six thousand unique products, was blaming new product development for complicating their lives. On top of this, a global shortage of IV solution was creating a major challenge for health-care systems around the world. The prospect of running out of this life-sustaining fluid had caused leading media outlets to unfairly blame their own organization, which was one of the world's largest producers of IV solution. As for the CEO, he was convinced that "if we had reinvested fifty percent of our profits back into future products, we probably could have avoided this present predicament."

When the CEO finished, he turned the meeting over to us. We began by saying, "We've spent time talking to several of you over the past few weeks, and here's our assessment: You are presently mired Below the Line. Until you decide to stop blaming your circumstances for your poor profit performance and start taking accountability for what happens next, we will see nothing but failure on this front in the future." These words hung in the air as a deafening silence fell over the room. It was clear no one had expected this sort of brutally frank assessment.

At that point, we sat back and silently waited for the team to respond. All eyes focused on the CEO. What would he say about what we said? He remained silent for a full minute, apparently deep in thought. Then he grinned, looked around the room, and in a rich German accent said, "You know, they're right." No one protested, no one defended his or her lack of leadership, and every head in the room began to nod. The CEO flashed us a thumbs-up. "Thank you. Please continue."

We dedicated the remaining time in our meeting to exploring the Steps to Accountability model and discussing specific ways the team could use it to get back Above the Line. It all boiled down to asking and answering the four essential questions we address more fully in chapters 3, 4, 5, and 6:

1. Have I acknowledged the full reality of this situation? (See It)
2. What have I done to contribute to this reality? (Own It)
3. What else can I do? (Solve It)
4. Who will do what by when? (Do It)

It took several hours of honest and vigorous discussion to address these questions, but before the meeting ended, each executive had moved Above the Line. They pinpointed specific adjustments each of them could make in his or her area of responsibility. A new sense of urgency consumed the leaders along with a firm resolve to achieve their key profit result. Their to-do list included:

1. spreading the sense of urgency to the managing directors who reported to them,
2. tightening controls on accounts payable and accounts receivable,
3. making large orders and shipments the top priority over the subsequent four weeks, and
4. speeding up the delivery of all orders through a central processing center.

Each of these initiatives was directed at achieving the key profit result and moving the company forward. The president of the North American region told us later that evening as he was driving us down the Autobahn at well over 120 miles per hour to the next event, "It took a lot of guts to call out an entire executive team like that, but it's exactly what we needed to get us to own and change our reality. We turned an important corner today."

Getting Accountability Right: The Fundamentals Matter

1. The CEO of a major consumer products company uses the Steps to Accountability model for an easy reference guide to taking accountability for Key Results. He refers to it often during one-on-ones with his direct reports and others. No one is able to offer excuses in his office without receiving a review of the Steps model.

2. The chief human resources officer of a massive health-care system rewrote the hiring guidelines for her company to include an intense focus on taking accountability for the company's two patient-centered Key Results.

3. One CEO makes sure his direct reports apply the Steps to Accountability model to themselves regularly by having each of them acknowledge what took them Below the Line during the past week and what they did to get back Above the Line.

4. Our client leaders learn to effectively apply accountability as a powerful, propelling force for achieving Key Results. They recognize that people spend far more time Below the Line than they realize. And they quickly acknowledge when they slip Below the Line and refuse to allow themselves to get stuck there.

Chapter Two

KEY RESULTS

Defining and Achieving What Matters Most

Creating accountability begins with clearly defining results. Clearly defined and well-understood results are those select, few deliverables that every individual in the organization is aligned around and committed to achieve, no matter his or her role, function, department, or geographical location. We refer to these select, few deliverables as *Key Results*. Ideally, Key Results should be limited to three to five meaningful, measurable, and memorable outcomes. Without such clarity and specificity, alignment suffers, and accountability is marginalized throughout the organization.

Here's what we mean by meaningful, measurable, and memorable.

- Meaningful: Key Results are so important that every individual employed by the organization must be able to connect his or her day-to-day work with each and every key result. For example, a 3 percent increase in profit margin as a Key Result would be meaningful if every single employee were able to connect his or her individual impact on that Key Result every single day through priority setting and decision making. Sometimes the linkage to the Key Result is indirect, but making the link is critical. If an organization had a Key Result of 5 percent revenue growth, someone working in a front-line HR role would need to understand how the business practices they employ can better align with and support the delivery of that Key Result.

• Measurable: Each Key Result should be captured and framed by a single category, metric, and target. While most categories will never find the perfect single metric, committing to and then leading an entire organization to hit one less-than-perfect metric and target is more effective than committing to and leading an entire organization in pursuit of some fifteen metrics for each respective category. In the example above, profit margin is the category, percentage increase is the metric, and 3 percent increase for the year is the target.

• Memorable: First and foremost, there should be no more than three to five Key Results. Additionally, when the Key Results are captured in a single-word label or simple phrase, people in the organization pay more attention and remember. The fewer the words, the stickier and more memorable the result. For example, we had one *Fortune* 1000 client that used three numbers to capture the organization's three Key Results: 5/10/1. The 5 represented the desired percentage of top-line revenue growth, 10 represented the desired percentage of bottom-line profit growth, and 1 percent represented the desired percentage of total manufacturing cost reduction. Tens of thousands of employees used those three numbers to guide their actions and decisions every single business day of the calendar year.

Clarity around Key Results allows every individual in the organization to clearly identify "My Impact" on the Key Results. It also drastically reduces the amount of time people spend debating priorities and resource allocation. Key Results provide a common lens for individuals and teams. Clarity around Key Results helps propel people to rise above their circumstances, overcome obstacles, break through cross-functional boundaries, and continually ask, "What else can I (we) do?" until they actually deliver what matters most.

Can You State Your Organization's Short List of Key Results?

Partners In Leadership (PIL) worked with Elaine Ullian when she was CEO of Boston Medical Center (BMC). As we began our first conference call with her, we exchanged a few pleasantries and then dove into the agenda. It didn't take long for us to appreciate Elaine's quick wit and unique business acumen.

PIL: "What Key Results does Boston Medical Center need to deliver in the next twelve to twenty-four months?"

Elaine didn't skip a beat: "We have a balanced scorecard."

PIL: "Great. What's on the scorecard?"

Elaine: "Hold on a second while I find it." Then she rattled off twenty-one individual measures from the scorecard before we asked her to pause.

PIL: "How many results are there on the scorecard?"

Elaine: "Four."

PIL: "But you've already identified over twenty."

Elaine: "Well, we have four buckets."

PIL: "So, you have a number of measures in each bucket?"

Elaine: "Yes."

PIL: "How many buckets have we covered so far?"

Elaine: "Um, the first one."

PIL: "How many measures are there in each of the buckets?"

Elaine: "They are all about the same as the one I just described."

PIL: "So that means you're asking your people to focus on eighty-plus results?"

Elaine: "Well, yes. But it doesn't sound very good when you say it like that. Let me explain. . . ."

Elaine then described all the ways BMC kept people on track, from state-of-the-art digital dashboards to frequent executive team and town hall staff meetings where progress on their results was thoroughly scrutinized.

We congratulated her for placing so much emphasis on results, thanked her for taking time out of her hectic schedule to chat with us, and said we'd get back to her after we had interviewed each member of her executive leadership team.

Not surprisingly, the interviews went much the same way. We asked each executive about the Key Results that BMC needed to achieve. Each time the leader pulled out a binder or handful of papers and started reading aloud the list of results until we asked them to pause. "Rather than read the list, can you tell us from memory what's contained in the scorecard?" The answers varied from three to five out of the eighty-plus measures. Predictably, no two lists matched perfectly. The CFO's list emphasized financial measures; the HR director's list stressed staff engagement; and leaders on the clinical side of the business put safety and quality measures first and foremost.

A week later we opened a follow-up call with Elaine by asking: "How many of the eighty-plus results do you think your executive team remembered without reading them off the master list?" After several quiet moments on the line, a nervous laugh broke the silence. The point had been made. Elaine, to her great credit, quickly acknowledged that even she, as the CEO, could give us no more than a handful of results accurately from memory.

We then put Elaine at ease by pointing out that we encountered this challenge all the time. A company sets its sights on a bunch of goals designed to guide as many employees as possible and then leaves it up to its people to figure out the three to five most important ones they need to deliver. Over the next hour we demonstrated the power of bringing clarity and alignment by focusing on three to five major outcomes that defined success for the entire medical center.

Elaine got it and embraced it.

About a year into the engagement at BMC, Elaine shared with us her new philosophy around Key Results: "It's really quite simple. You need to choose them wisely, distribute them widely, focus on them relentlessly, and measure your progress toward them all the time. That's the only way to take accountability for the results you need." She became a champion of simplicity and a master at creating alignment and accountability for the achievement of BMC's Key Results. Both Elaine and her team went on to create unprecedented focus and clarity across the system, leading to dramatic improvements in patient volume, safety, satisfaction, and cost control. BMC's four Key Results became known as VSSC (pronounced "visk")—volume, safety, satisfaction, and cost—and produced a rallying cry that united and aligned the entire organization around what was most important for BMC's growth and success.

Key Results Principles

A culture wherein you get accountability right is created and sustained by applying four fundamental principles:

1. Define Key Results to Promote Accountability and Facilitate Needed Change.

2. Create Joint Accountability to Improve the Probability of Achieving Key Results.
3. Realize that Working to Achieve Key Results Is the Essence of Working Above the Line.
4. Ring the Bell of Success as Progress Is Made to Keep People Focused on Their Impact.

Let's examine each of these principles in detail.

1. Define Key Results to Promote Accountability and Facilitate Needed Change

You will recall that in chapter 1 we offered *The Oz Principle* definition of accountability. It's worth repeating here:

> A personal choice to rise above one's circumstances and demonstrate the ownership necessary for achieving desired results; to See It, Own It, Solve It, and Do It.

Note, again, the purposeful emphasis and focus on desired results. As leaders clearly define a manageable number of meaningful, measurable, and memorable Key Results, individuals are actually empowered to take accountability to look at what else they can do to achieve them. Nine out of ten senior management teams fail to clearly define their Key Results. Their failure to do so prevents people from looking at what else they can do to achieve them. People cannot take accountability for the undefined. So, what happens?

They simply put their heads down and focus on doing the activities associated with their jobs, irrespective of the connection between those activities and Key Results.

Do you remember the last time you were asked, "What's your job?" All of us get that question in one form or another from time to time. Think about your typical response. First, we usually state our title. Then, we quickly realize that our titles often don't mean much to those outside our organization, so we summarize our job description. But what's in our job description? Invariably it's a list of activities. Unfortunately, "doing the job" often means focusing on a flurry of activity that may or may not produce the desired results. Here's a quick example. A few years ago, we worked with a world-famous motorcycle manufacturer. Before we started our work, we interviewed some front-line employees. As we asked welders at the Kansas City plant "What's your job?" we consistently heard, "I am a welder and my job is to weld handlebars to front forks." After we worked with people at the plant for a month, we did another round of interviews. Here's what we heard from the welders in round two of our interviews: "My job is to deliver fifty bikes a day. I do that by completing two hundred and twelve welds with zero defects per eight-hour shift." Obviously, prior to their introduction to the Key Results, the welders were focused on just doing their jobs. Subsequent to the training and after a deliberate focus was created on their Key Results, they saw their jobs differently. It's not that their jobs got bigger; it's that they became accountable for something bigger than their jobs—the Key Results!

Returning to Elaine, the CEO at BMC, and her scorecard with her eighty different metrics, we found that, fortunately, Elaine was able to see the problem and chose to own it. Together with her leadership team they worked to align themselves and the entire BMC organization around their four Key Results: volume, safety, satisfaction, and cost control (VSSC). The impact, as we mentioned, was immediate. Aligned around the Key Results, leaders and individuals alike began asking what else they could do to achieve them. For instance, the team quickly determined that in order to achieve patient volume they had to reduce Emergency Room Diversion by 33 percent. Riveted on achieving patient volume, they vigorously explored what else they could do to reduce the number of times an ambulance needed to be redirected to a competing hospital because BMC was incapable of handling more patients.

As team members applied See It, Own It, Solve It, and Do It, they found numerous innovative ways to achieve the 33 percent reduction. For example, the outpatient clinics, generally located in an office park, were open Monday through Friday, from 9:00 a.m. to 5:00 p.m. We were in a meeting where we asked the clinics' managers to state the connection between their operation and BMC's current rate of Emergency Room Diversion, they simply responded, "That's not our job. We're four miles away from the hospital, and we're not open on weekends or late at night; we don't deal with emergencies."

As we pursued the dialogue further, we called upon a bright, young clinic manager who exclaimed, "Our outpatient clinics *do* impact ER Diversion. We regularly fall behind in our schedule and end up with two or three untreated patients needing to be rescheduled. These patients are sitting in our office waiting to be seen, but we tell them to come back the next day or the day after that. If it's a Friday, we tell them to come back on Monday." She continued by asking, "What do people in pain or alarmed by a medical problem do if an outpatient clinic tells them to go home and come back later?" Continuing, she said, "They drive four miles to the nearest hospital and sign up for treatment in the emergency room." Picture the scene in the emergency room: dozens of true emergency-level patients, some of them accident victims rushed to the hospital, plus scores of nonemergency-level patients turned away from the outpatient clinics. Talk to the emergency room nurses, and they'll say, "It's amazing. Like clockwork we get slammed every weekday at five thirty."

The connection was starting to sink in for the staff at the clinics. One of the leaders stated it perfectly: "When we fail to take accountability for our calendar, we clog up the ER with nonemergency patients and create ER Diversion." When everyone finally started talking about this issue and taking accountability to deliver on BMC's Key Results, they ended up making meaningful changes to their outpatient scheduling protocol. Within two months, BMC had reduced system-wide ER Diversion by 28 percent.

The impact on an organization where individuals take accountability to achieve the Key Results cannot be overstated. Teams galvanize around purpose. Cross-functional priorities that are aligned around a common purpose fuel collaboration. Motivation and resolve are deepened. Engagement and being proactive at every level improve. Resource allocation is facilitated with greater clarity. Responsiveness to customer needs accelerates. New-product and service innovation is heightened. Quality of products and services improves. Helping everyone see the connection between what he or she does all day long and how it impacts the team's ability to achieve the Key Results is critical to any organization's success. Do it well and you lay the groundwork for joint accountability for results.

2. Create Joint Accountability to Improve the Probability of Achieving Key Results

Since achieving Key Results almost always requires a concerted effort by more than one person, success depends on shared ownership and joint accountability. When individuals on a team choose to go Below the Line and begin pointing the finger at "Jack," for example, they ignore an opportunity to see their own accountability for the current situation and lose the chance to grow from the experience. Of course, you may breathe a sigh of relief when people agree that it's not Jack's fault, but that moment will be short lived. The organization still needs to achieve the Key Results. You're back to square one and perhaps without Jack's help. When an organization fails to reach its important goals, the lack of performance represents a collective, not an individual, failure.

A number of years ago Ryan Millar decided to join our company. Before joining our team, Ryan played middle blocker on three different US Olympic Men's Volleyball teams, including the gold medal team that competed at the Beijing Olympics. He has often talked about the mind-set required for six players to cover the entire volleyball court effectively, with each player assuming responsibility for a specific area that overlaps with the areas other players must cover. At any moment your defined responsibility might need to change in order to ensure the desired outcome. Ryan summed it up with a compelling story:

"We were up against Brazil, the defending Olympic champions and number one team in the world. Brazil served us the ball. One of our players passed the ball to our setter. Our setter directed the ball to one of our hitters, who crushed it over to the Brazilian defense. The Brazilians expertly defended the ball back over to our side of the net at me. I hit it back at them."

That was a defining moment in the match. Ryan's job as middle blocker was to block and hit back any ball that entered his sphere of responsibility in the middle of the court. He did just that. But then the Brazilians fired back a hard shot at Ryan, who suddenly found himself in an unaccustomed role. He was a blocker, not a setter.

"At that moment my job was to ensure we win the match by stepping outside of the job and into the setter role to deliver a perfect set to a teammate. I made the set. My teammate hit the ball back over the net for a winning point. The rest is history. If I had only worried about my own 'job,' blocking and hitting in the middle of the court, we might never have gotten our gold medal result."

When you get a workforce asking the question "What else can I do?" to achieve the result, especially during times of uncertainty, stress, challenge, or difficulty, magic can happen. That's the power of joint accountability. A serious complaint about equipment failure comes into the customer care call center of an industrial equipment manufacturer. The rep fielding the call may be able to resolve the issue, but he may also need to refer it to engineering for evaluation and repair or to sales for further investigation and replacement. Who bears responsibility for solving the problem doesn't matter as much as the need for someone, anyone, to solve it in a way that delights the customer.

One of our clients, the president of a well-known financial services company, described her frustration with the lack of joint accountability this way: "Everyone works hard so that we don't drop the ball; but when it does get dropped, too many people see the ball hit the ground and say, 'Hey,' pointing at a team member, 'you dropped the ball. It landed in *your* court.'" This client knew that projects can and do incur a lot of dropped balls. Someone misses a critical deadline, someone racks up an unexpected expense, someone overlooks a crucial detail or quits in the middle of an important task. Her frustration came when she observed how it was that her team reacted to the balls that were dropped. She saw people dive Below the Line and start playing the blame game rather than jumping Above the Line to See It, Own It, Solve It, and Do It!

Over the years we have asked many teams, "Who's accountable for quality?" In many organizations the response is fairly consistent: One hand goes up and everyone else in the room points at that person. Eventually, when we ask the question, "Who's accountable for quality?" every single hand goes up. People get joint accountability. As more companies move from awareness of joint accountability to implementation of joint accountability, improved results always follow.

A large manufacturer in the Midwest hired us to help implement an ambitious information technology initiative that would achieve system-wide integration of all of the company's vital information. It was a huge and complex undertaking. Since the senior executives knew it would push people to their limit, they hoped to make it easier by assembling a team that included skilled people from every major organizational function. The individuals brought very different backgrounds and functional responsibilities to the project, and none had ever participated in such a massive IT project. Making matters worse, they knew that previous, smaller IT initiatives had overshot their budgets and schedules. That history of delays and cost overruns made them doubt their ability to bring this massive project in on time and on budget. Getting this large and varied group of people to work together was a daunting task.

During the project kickoff meeting, we worked with the team to define and create accountability for the behaviors and attitudes needed to accomplish the mission within a year. At the outset, senior leadership carefully linked the project to the company's three Key Results:

1. Growing revenue by 25 percent over the next twenty-four months
2. Scaling up manufacturing by 25 percent in twelve months to meet increased demand
3. Increasing surveyed customer satisfaction by 25 percent

The new system needed to pump out more product to fulfill increased demand. If the team couldn't make that happen, they risked creating a lot of unhappy customers. Their whole brand could suffer as a result. In a very real sense, our client was betting the farm on this project. Timing was crucial. The increase in demand would occur in twelve months, at which time the new system needed to be fully up and running. Success depended on the alignment of the team and a deep sense of joint accountability for the newly clarified

Key Results. They needed everyone to continually ask what else they could do to solve the problems they would face along the way, overcome the obstacles that would arise, and, ultimately, achieve the Key Results. It worked. People constantly referred to "the Line," coaching teammates who sank below it and urging them to get back above it. When the following year rolled around, the system was humming like a well-oiled machine. It came in not only ahead of schedule but also under budget. For years to come, that project served as a model for every other strategic initiative.

Joint accountability often requires that a company dismantle its silos and create cross-functional teams. Legendary General Electric CEO Jack Welch strove hard to create what he called a "boundary-less" organization. "If this company is to achieve its goals, we've all got to become boundaryless. Boundaries are crazy. The [labor] union is just another boundary, and you have to reach across the same way you want to reach across the boundaries separating you from your customers and your suppliers and your colleagues."

Here's another case in point. We were engaged by one of the largest global manufacturers of dishwashers and other home appliances. One of the company's plants ran two parallel assembly lines separated by a row of inventory-handling offices and storage units. Each line functioned autonomously for the most part, and each had developed its own unique culture. Under the leadership of the line supervisor, the workers on Assembly One became adept at quickly identifying a faulty subassembly from any one of the twenty workstations on the line. When someone identified a bad subassembly, the supervisor immediately confronted the operator responsible for the problem and, with everyone watching, embarrassed that person into correcting the problem and improving future performance. Naturally, everyone else on the line, protected by an illusion of safety, would blame the erring operator for slowing them down. Over time, however, people began hiding their mistakes, hoping to remain sheltered from blame, and would not acknowledge an error even when confronted by the supervisor. As a result, production output had been declining and defective subassemblies and scrap had been increasing for several months.

Next door on Assembly Two the workers had developed a markedly different kind of culture. When an operator made a mistake at a workstation, other workers would immediately offer help in solving the problem quickly and without a lot of discussion. Functioning as part of a team, each worker felt jointly accountable for the end result of assembling quality products on time. Free from the false illusion of safety created by explanations and victim stories, the workers appreciated and helped one another, quickly identifying mistakes but never accusing one individual of hurting the group effort. As a result, production on the second assembly line remained high, with fewer defective subassemblies and scrap near zero levels.

The workers on Assembly One were hiding their errors, blaming each other for mistakes, and generally walking, talking, and thinking like victims. In contrast, the workers on Assembly Two enjoyed their work, liked working with each other, felt fulfilled, and produced great results. What was the difference between these two work cultures? We see one fundamental difference between the two: One work culture demonstrated joint accountability for results and stayed Above the Line; the other did not.

3. Realize that Working to Achieve Key Results Is the Essence of Working Above the Line

When someone is stuck Below the Line, what are they actually trying to achieve? Not the Key Results. When people get stuck Below the Line they have given up on the results and are now working on the story they can tell to justify why they can't do it. Taking accountability always poses a certain amount of personal risk. "I'm just doing my job" creates a comfort zone, but that comfort zone often threatens your ability to get results. The comfort it provides is an illusion. Overcoming that illusion requires taking accountability for owning "My Impact" on achieving the Key Results, which only happens Above the Line.

Consider the case of Dennis Antinori, the vice president of sales for a large medical products company, who anxiously awaited an upcoming national sales meeting at which the company would launch several new products. Two months before the meeting, Dennis received word that the new products would arrive a full twelve months late. Stunned by the news, he struggled with three enormous challenges:

1. how to hit his numbers without the help of new products,
2. how to help his sales management team stay Above the Line, and
3. how to keep his sales reps committed to achieving their sales targets despite the lack of new products.

Having learned to operate Above the Line and view accountability as a powerful, positive force, Dennis met with his sales managers to take a new look at their circumstances. After setting his watch for twenty minutes and letting the team spend some therapeutic time Below the Line in the victim cycle, complaining about why they felt let down by the rest of the company, Dennis consciously moved the discussion Above the Line. Viewed from Above the Line, the huge obstacles to achieving sales targets still looked formidable but not insurmountable. Dennis asked: "Given the obstacles we face, and they are huge, what else can we do to rise above them and achieve the results we want, and the company needs?" At first the question baffled the sales managers. "How," they asked, "do you solve a new-products problem without new products?" Dennis shot back, "That's not our *real* problem. The *real* problem is a sales problem, not a new-products problem. We must accept the reality that we will receive no new products this year and that the company still needs us to hit its numbers. Assigning blame to the new-product development folks won't remove our responsibility to deliver on targeted sales." After a lengthy discussion, the team climbed Above the Line and began asking: "What else can we do to achieve this year's sales targets, despite not having any new products?"

In the months following this meeting, Dennis Antinori and his sales management team found many new and creative ways to boost sales and meet the targets set at the beginning of the year. By year's end they turned in an outstanding performance, one of the best in the history of the company: a healthy 15 percent increase in sales over the previous year. After the year ended, Dennis asked his team: "What most contributed to our sales success last year?" Here's how he summarized their responses: "Everyone felt that we took an Above the Line approach to the situation. We wasted little time blaming new-product development and challenged ourselves to stop all negative thinking. Then we put our heads together to come up with solutions we may not have considered before. We met the challenge head-on. We got focused rather than frustrated, and we made it happen despite the odds stacked against us."

When leaders clearly define the Key Results their team or organization needs to produce, they not only commence the all-important effort of connecting every single person to what matters most, but they also shatter the illusion that busyness, routine activity, micromanaging every little detail of work, or going through the motions is "doing the job." Doing the job is achieving the result. What costs an organization more, a momentary setback when a creative solution fails and sends you back to the drawing board or the permanent paralysis of victimhood? It's no sin to go back to the drawing board if doing so drives you toward Key Results; but it is delusional to keep running in place like a hamster inside a fast-turning wheel assuming progress is happening. Effective leaders teach their people about the true costs of Below the Line thinking and behavior, while stressing the benefits of getting and staying Above the Line.

4. Ring the Bell of Success as Progress Is Made to Keep People Focused on Their Impact

When everyone shares accountability for achieving organizational results, they almost automatically create momentum and speed toward achieving Key Results. Each and every person embraces the same definition of a successful future, sees a connection between their specific job and where the organization needs to go, and feels invested in the cause to get there. We always suggest that leaders "ring a bell" that signals achievements along the road to results. It can take many forms, be it an actual bell or something else that provides meaningful recognition. Without clear reminders of progress, people can get lost in the daily activity it takes to do their jobs and lose their focus on results. Recognizing positive performance wherever and whenever it shows up creates momentum and reinforces the importance of taking personal and joint accountability for what matters most. We all know that in sports, players gain extra energy and commitment when they see the scoreboard light up and hear their fans cheering from the grandstands when they score points.

One of our clients, the newly appointed leader of a large international sales force, quickly discovered that his sales force focused primarily on daily tasks. Those who were traveling extensively and those who worked primarily in the office felt worn down by the daily grind and tended to do little more than go through the motions until they arrived home and could relax. How could he combat that fatigue and instill renewed excitement around closing sales and achieving a 25 percent increase in total gross sales? He needed something more than the year-end bonuses to keep his people fired up along the way. Eventually, he came up with a little idea that might make a big difference. He installed a large bronze bell on the wall outside his office. Throughout the day, when an in-house or traveling rep closed a sale, the bell would ring so loudly people could hear it throughout the entire floor of offices and cubicles.

As you might imagine, the bell caught people's attention, not only in the sales force but throughout the company as well. Before long, everyone began to work hard to do something that would merit ringing the bell. Because it was rung for a specific act that moved the organization in the direction it needed to go, it automatically reinforced the need to look beyond processes, procedures, and policies to focus, instead, on the Key Results the sales force needed to achieve. Whether you were traveling or in the office, you always heard or heard about the bell ringing.

You'll want to establish your own "bell-ringing" practice at the beginning of a new fiscal year, during the launch of a major new project or initiative, and whenever you propose a new set of Key Results. People need to see more than the goal line; they also need to hear the bell that marks a significant step toward it. The more it rings, the more momentum you'll create. "The bell" helps people focus on the Key Results and avoid getting lost in the forest of activity. When the bell keeps ringing, it reinforces the sort of accountability that creates momentum and breeds success.

Getting Accountability Right: Clearly Define Results and Put Them Front and Center

1. A chief information officer of an insurance company began his staff meetings by quizzing people on the Key Results, asking for members of the team to "make the link" between their jobs and each of the Key Results. He often rewarded strong answers with Starbucks gift cards.
2. The communications team of a major energy producer outside of Philadelphia placed large billboards of their Key Results

along the mile-long drive up to the parking lot at their head-quarters. The first billboard meant to tee up the others was a bit smaller and read: "Your job is to achieve . . ."

3. A large retail client decided to formalize meeting agendas across the entire organization. One aspect of the standard meeting agenda template was to separate and categorize agenda items using the Key Results. The simple message was, If you can't connect the agenda item to a Key Result, it won't make it onto our agenda!

4. We worked with a large car manufacturer (*Fortune* 50) that integrated its three Key Results of "Three Zeros" (emissions, accidents, congestion) into virtually everything it did. These Key Results became so integrated and inspiring that front-line union workers would often reference the key deliverables on their own.

Chapter Three

SEE IT

Mustering the Courage to Acknowledge Reality

Seeing It is the first and the hardest step Above the Line. In fact, we would say that it is often a "showstopper" step for individuals, teams, and organizations as a whole. Seeing It requires a level of curiosity, courage, and humility that allows you to hear what you may be uncomfortable hearing. In order to fully See It you must be hungry for perspectives you don't already have, you must be able to face reality, and you must be willing to acknowledge that you don't have all the answers. Without curiosity, courage, and humility you will be severely limited in your ability to See It.

Acknowledging the reality of a situation, especially an unpleasant, upsetting, or unfair one, never comes easily. And because See It requires a certain level of humility that experienced and novice leaders alike often lose during their rise to positions of power in the organization, this step can become a serious obstacle to a leader's continued effectiveness. Oftentimes leaders begin thinking they must be the ones to provide all the answers. However, in our experience, the most effective leaders create space for others to fill. They see things more clearly by reaching out and seeking the perspectives of others. They are curious and reflect a sincere desire to see what others see. They know of the material impact that these other perspectives will have on their ability to fully grasp what's going on. On the other hand, the least effective leaders we interact with take up all the space. They already have all the answers. Their perspective is the one that counts. This debilitating mind-set keeps them from obtaining needed information and prevents them from acknowledging the reality of any given situation—they just won't See It.

No one sees everything perfectly, but you can get a lot closer to seeing things as they really are by reaching out and obtaining the perspectives of others. To do this, you must be open to the possibility that you may not see some important aspects of your organization's reality.

It takes real effort to look past your own limited perspective to see what others are seeing.

What Are You Not Seeing?

It took a lot of hard work to transform a major equipment manufacturer's sluggish "Ignore and Deny" culture into a more robust one, in which Seeing It became a daily habit, and it all started with the CEO acknowledging the company's reality. His first year as CEO was no cakewalk. With fifteen deaths tied to equipment failures, a

wave of product recalls, and a $50 million fine, the company's repu-
tation had taken a beating. The CEO found himself in the middle of
a tornado of bad publicity and customer outrage on the day he took
his seat in the corner office. Having suffered through a bankruptcy
earlier in his career, he was not about to let that calamity imperil
this company.

From the start, the CEO deftly confronted the problems plaguing the company with remarkable transparency and openness. Soon
after he began his tenure as CEO, he decisively dismissed fifteen
workers in the wake of an investigation into the product recall. Then
he immediately adopted a digital media communications strategy
that used multiple platforms to deliver an authentic, humble, and
genuine message: "Problems don't go away when you ignore them;
they get bigger." He was telling the world, "I *see it*. I'll deal with it
head-on."

His performance in the top job at the company prompted an
industry magazine to put his name atop its list of the most successful
turnaround CEOs. In no small part, he earned that honor because
he demanded that people speak up the instant they saw problems
occurring anywhere in the organization. Specifically, he was telling
people:

When you See It, Say It.

We helped the CEO craft one of his company's most vital cultural beliefs: "Be Bold: I respectfully speak up and share ideas without fear." With boldness and dedicated courage, the CEO launched

an era of change at the equipment manufacturer that transformed the company from a place where fearful people kept their eyes closed and their mouths shut to one where everyone strove to see and talk about any issue that impeded the company's ability to achieve better results.

See It Principles

Andrew S. Grove, former chairman of Intel, understood a common risk posed to virtually every business: "Every company faces a critical point when it must change dramatically to rise to the next level of performance. If the company fails to *see* and *seize* that moment, it will start to decline. The key is courage."

Acknowledging Below the Line behavior and facing up to the reality of a situation should be rewarded, not punished. As we discussed in chapter 1, accountability isn't a hammer for punishing people who have failed; it's an engine that propels people toward greater personal growth and better results. We humans are by nature flawed. Ignoring our flaws gets us nowhere; acknowledging them helps us more clearly see our situation and the path toward better results. The founder and CEO of a major health-care system reaffirmed this timeless truth in his closing remarks after a two-day leadership meeting we had facilitated. He told his team, "I want to leave you with a thought I can't get out of my mind: I now have to face the disgusting and inconvenient truth that it's now all about *me* changing!"

These four See It principles will help you begin to change what needs changing:

1. Park Your Ego at the Door to Improve Your Vision.
2. Welcome Difficult Conversations to Make Them Contagious.
3. Embrace the Feedback You Receive to Accelerate Your Ability to Change.
4. Link What You See to Key Results to Keep You on the Path to Achieving Them.

Let's look at each principle more closely.

1. Park Your Ego at the Door to Improve Your Vision

Egotism is a choice one makes to place themselves at the center of their world and focus almost exclusively on satisfying their own needs and welfare first. This choice keeps people from seeing the full picture. Some leaders, for example, find it difficult to deal with millennials, precisely because they see the world so differently. There are those of the boomer generation or the one that followed in its footsteps, Gen X, who have held the perception that millennials act like self-absorbed children who are allergic to hard work and feel entitled to rewards and promotions without earning them. Leaders who let these views dictate the way they relate to millennials or the Gen Zers try to impose their ideas on the future leaders of their organizations rather than hear them, learn from them, and take advantage of the obvious differences. As boomers choose to see beyond the stereotypes of the younger generations, they discover a treasure trove of highly talented people with unique dreams and aspirations to which they are passionately committed. Here are a few current facts that support the need to understand and embrace these differences:

- In 2018 millennials surpassed baby boomers and Gen Xers as the largest demographic in the US workforce.
- According to research published by Gallup, 71 percent of millennials are passively or actively *disengaged* at work.
- The same study showed that 60 percent of millennials are strongly considering new employment opportunities right now.
- The 29 percent of millennials who *are* engaged at work said they are less likely to switch jobs if the job market improved in the next twelve months.
- Eighty-two percent of millennials claim loyalty to their employers.
- Only 1 percent of HR professionals believe that millennials feel loyal to their employers.

Do you see both the paradox and opportunity here? When millennials, or in fact any other employees, do not fully engage in their work, productivity suffers. Results fall short of expectations. In addition to the decline in productivity, consider the cost of high employee turnover. Recent studies reported by *Training Industry* and the Association for Talent Development (ATD) estimate the cost can run as high as $25,000 per job hopper. Some researchers offer an even higher average cost of turnover. For more than thirty years Partners In Leadership has researched and studied the topic of workplace engagement and disengagement. We can boil our findings down to one deceptively simple rule:

If you want to increase workforce engagement,
ensure everyone knows you hear their voices.

Engaging workers requires that leaders set aside any preference for the outdated "command and control" or "the boss knows best" style of management. While some may still cling to many of those post–World War II practices, a military-like approach to managing people simply does not work with subsequent generations of workers. What works is to park your ego at the door and create an environment of trust where people, young and old, receive the respect they deserve.

2. Welcome Difficult Conversations to Make Them Contagious

When coaching clients on taking the See It step, we offer three major suggestions: "Dialogue, dialogue, and dialogue." We were recently helping the Global Leadership Team of a Fortune 500 multimedia company orchestrate a multiday event. The CEO of one of the biggest food and beverage companies in the world and a key member of the board of directors kicked off the leadership conference. At the end of his speech, the CEO asked for questions. A hand shot up in a back corner of the room. "How does a multinational company like yours, with a lumbering footprint around the globe, accelerate the pace of change when you need to move quickly?"

"Good question." The CEO smiled and paused while everyone waited for an answer that was sure to involve the latest thinking in change management from the Ivy Leagues. But that didn't come! Instead, he offered a deceptively simple answer:

"Today, if you are having the difficult conversations only once a year, you need to start having them twice a year. If you're already having the difficult conversations twice a year, start having them quarterly. If today you're having the difficult conversations quarterly, then start having them monthly. If you have them monthly already, start having them weekly. And if you already have the difficult conversations once a week, start having them daily." He then said, with emotion in his voice, "If you want to accelerate change, you have to compress the cycle time on your difficult conversations." We couldn't have said it better ourselves.

Leaders who follow this rule naturally model it for others, causing the whole culture to move toward operating in a "See It, Say It" mode. They foster a sense of trust in the culture. After assessing thousands of organizations over the past thirty years, we've arrived at an important insight:

Organizations that insist on frequent difficult conversations create the highest levels of accountability.

Candid and honest dialogue helps everyone to see the reality of a situation. It almost goes without saying that a willingness to ignore and deny the truth prevents people from Seeing It. Ernest Hemingway captured it perfectly in his 1926 novel *The Sun Also Rises:*

"How did you go bankrupt?" Bill asked.

"Two ways," Mike said. "Gradually and then suddenly."

How true! If you're not paying attention, an ignored truth or hard reality can sneak up on you until BAM! It knocks you off your feet. Do "candid and honest" occasionally, and you will go broke gradually, then suddenly. Do it all the time, and you will prosper. Kelli Valade's promotion to president of Chili's Grill & Bar shows the benefits of having open feedback ingrained as a habit.

In 2016, four decades after its founding in Dallas, Chili's Grill & Bar named Kelli Valade its first female president. Her new job put Kelli in charge of overseeing all aspects of domestic restaurant operations, marketing, franchising, and human resources for the brand, which operated roughly sixteen hundred restaurants at the time. Immediately after assuming the top job, she knew that effectively leading the company's far-flung network would depend on increasing the number of difficult conversations she and her people had. Wanting people to see and talk about and listen to observations about what was going right and wrong in the company, she formed what she called "Kelli's Councils." These councils, composed mostly of front-line staff and managers, became her operational eyes and ears. As she formed these councils within every region of the organization, she began learning about tactical problems that were occurring within the restaurants' day-to-day operations. This early warning system enabled her to streamline operations and increase revenue quickly, thereby demonstrating to the entire organization that "feedback is priceless," a mantra Kelli recited to her people every day.

3. Embrace the Feedback You Receive to Accelerate Your Ability to Change

Several years ago, we began working with a global fast-food concept that was hemorrhaging market share to its competitors. The company had pioneered an approach to franchising that stimulated such rapid and expansive growth that the company had dominated its segment for decades. Over time, however, leadership had grown complacent. In the eyes of customers, the product had changed very little and now seemed very similar to competitors' offerings. As a result, the brand was losing a lot of its once-loyal fans. Ironically, their competitors had mimicked their own business model so well that its once formidable strategy no longer offered superior value. Their market share dipped, and the stock price withered.

During one of our initial interactions with their expanded leadership team, the company's CEO introduced us at the meeting by saying, "Before we get into the topic of this morning's meeting, I want to play a short video for you." This was news to us. As we watched the screen, we were surprised to see the face of Jim Cramer, the brash, fast-talking host of the show *Mad Money* on CNBC. For six full minutes Cramer tore apart the leadership team seated in the room. He bemoaned the arrogance displayed by senior leaders when he interviewed them. He derided their excuse making for the company's current plight. He sneered at the fact that they blamed their poor performance on a weak economy and the competition's aggressive pricing tactics. It all boiled down to one sad conclusion: The brand's leaders had become master players of the blame game.

Cramer then went on to compare their financials to those of a competitor that had been eating their lunch the past few years. In talks with that rival, Cramer didn't hear a single discouraging word. Cramer described how every conversation he had, he was hearing great strategic thinking around new products built for the current economic realities and innovative approaches to creating greater internal efficiencies and a better customer experience.

The video clip ended with Cramer picking up one of the brand's once-praised products lying on a table in his studio set, then throwing it against the wall and watching it slowly slide to the floor as he proclaimed, "There's your stock price!" And then, rubbing a little salt in the wound, he said that the company was shedding crocodile tears about its competitive environment, its competition was taking accountability for its circumstances and not letting the recent downturn in the fast-food industry detour the company off the road to better results.

Imagine the stunned silence when the screen went black. The CEO looked at the expanded team and said, "You know what? Cramer is right. I've been Below the Line as your CEO, and I've allowed you to go there with me."

He concluded his thoughts with a stern warning. "We need every single employee in this company knowing what it looks like to take accountability for our situation before it's too late! These folks are going to help us take greater personal, team, and organizational accountability for a better future." He then turned the meeting over to us. We welcomed the challenge.

Fast-forward: This brand started posting biting and harsh

comments about its product all over its offices to fuel and engage its need for change. After asking for and acting on an unprecedented amount of feedback for a full year, their leaders realized the power of carefully listening to employees and customers. They began to internalize and implement customer feedback as if it were manna from heaven. This feedback fueled changes to their overall product mix as well as ingredient overhauls with their core products. Over the course of a few years the company posted record top-line and bottom-line results.

Looking back on our experience with this impressive turn-around, we would attribute the company's change in trajectory to a basic (yet not-so-easy-to-acquire) new habit: constant, unrelenting feedback that kept its See It lens clear and sharply focused.

It takes patience, persistence, and courage
to ask for and listen to the hard truths.

We've said for years that Seeing It depends as much on your ears as on your eyes. As you come to understand that reality at your core, you will seek and provide feedback as if your life depends on it.

4. Link What You See to Key Results to Keep You on the Path to Achieve Them

You may see a lot of problems you think your organization should solve, but unless a given problem prevents you from achieving the Key Results you're seeking, you should not make it a top priority. As we discussed in chapter 2, you must both know and understand the Key Results, why they must be achieved, and whether or not specific problems need to be solved in order to achieve them.

There's no point in taking the next Steps to Accountability or solving a specific problem if it will not move the organization closer to its objectives. Before you proceed to the Own It step, make sure you fully understand, can clearly communicate, and fully grasp *why* the organization needs to achieve its Key Results.

If it doesn't link to a Key Result, it's not a top priority.

Six years ago, we worked with a huge multinational organization that manufactures consumer products all over the globe. Walk into any public restroom in the world and you're likely to see their products. The company's CEO had developed a strategic imperatives and priorities scorecard that listed two full pages of metrics and targets for every nook and cranny in the organization. The name of each member of the leadership team appeared on the scorecard with a number of specific items behind the name. For example, the VP of HR should improve the company's talent-recruiting process, the chief information officer should collapse the time frame it takes to get a new system up and running, the operations manager should implement an important new materials management system at each manufacturing facility, and the VP of finance should provide more detailed analyses of current cash flow practices.

"Well," said each leader, "I'll need to add more people to get that result." Unfortunately, the budget was already stretched to the breaking point. An all-out war broke out, with each leader defending his or her turf and battling for scarce resources.

That's when the CEO asked us for help. As we began interviewing the various leaders, it became quite clear that they were spending more time sabotaging each other's initiatives than striving to accomplish their own. Collaboration had sunk to an all-time low. Each leader protected his or her silo. No one at or below the VP level could clearly communicate the company's Key Results.

It was a classic case of "I can't see the forest for the trees." Everyone could cite a long list of problems that needed to get solved, but the sheer number of priorities kept people from seeing the most important results. The leaders could not link what they were seeing to the company's Key Results because the CEO had created far too many priorities and had failed to communicate what the company absolutely, positively needed to accomplish this year. With our help, he identified a short list of must-do items. Then he convened a meeting at which he sent a clear message: "Forget about yourself, your management team, and your functional area for a moment and think like a CEO. Ask yourself, 'What does this business really need to do to be successful?' Here's what I think." He passed out a short list:

Our Key Results

1. High Quality: No Product Returns
2. Safety: Zero Injuries
3. Profit Margin: 10 Percent
4. Employee Engagement: Reduce Voluntary Turnover by 15 Percent

"Will you help me figure out how your part of the organization will help us get there?"

Everyone felt a profound shift in the way they were looking at the company's future. They knew that if they could achieve those results, the company could thrive. They also knew that they needed to focus and solve any problem that got in the way of achieving those results. All the haggling over resources that had previously created friction came to a halt. As the senior team contemplated the short list of Key Results, people acknowledged that they had been "stuck in the weeds" and offered ideas on ways to get back to basics.

One year later the organization had not only achieved its Key Results but had also fixed many of the problems that previously plagued its teams. With everyone aligned around the Key Results, collaboration improved dramatically, and the old turf wars became ancient history. Feedback began to focus on progress made and progress needed. It was no longer an "interpersonal exchange," where any personal complaint could be aired. Instead, feedback became an "organizational conversation" that moved people more quickly toward achieving Key Results. In fact, open and candid feedback, clear and honest communication, and a willingness to admit personal fallibility became the hallmark of most meetings involving senior leadership.

Getting Accountability Right:
Stepping Up to See It

1. Ray Burick at Lockheed Martin created "Artisan Councils" where front-line workers were invited to share thoughts and ideas on how to impact their culture and deliver Key Results more efficiently. A "War Room" was created where feedback was posted on the walls and improvements were shared and tracked.

2. One executive of a *Fortune* 10 company sat on the stage for two hours eagerly seeking feedback on his own leadership from his top 350 leaders. Each piece of feedback he received was carefully recorded on a legal pad that was sitting on his lap. A week later one of the directors in the meeting told us that he never thought he'd live to see the day when an executive at his company would be so vulnerable, humble, and effective in opening up conversation about personal and organizational growth.

3. Ginger Graham, while CEO at Advanced Cardiovascular Systems, created "feedback relationships" between front-line employees and each member of her executive team. Ginger's feedback partner was Kevin, who worked on the company's shipping dock. Every month Ginger would meet with Kevin to seek feedback from him about his view of the company. This experience was so meaningful for Ginger that she would later feature some of what she learned from Kevin's feedback in an article titled "If You Want Honesty, Break Some Rules," published in the *Harvard Business Review*. In the article she referenced not only the value of the feedback she received from

Kevin but also the impact of the stories shared throughout her organization that related to the unique interaction that senior executives had with front-line employees.

4. One client, who happened to be a prominent manufacturer of competitive golf clubs, created a simple scorecard to track weekly feedback exchanges. Much like you'd track your own score when playing golf, this company created a mentality within its culture that "if you're going to improve at something, you better be able to measure and track progress along the way." The company's leaders shared with us that in their first few weeks of implementing the scorecard they tracked thousands of feedback exchanges that would not have otherwise occurred.

Chapter Four

OWN IT

Assessing Agreement and Defining Involvement

People tend to care more about what they own than what they do not. Most of us will take better care of a car we've purchased with our hard-earned money than we will a rental car. The same applies to business situations. If you or your team start to fall short of achieving Key Results, your personal ownership will determine the lengths to which you will go to correct the situation. Once you See It—that is, the reality of your own, your team's, and/or your organization's situation—you may be tempted to not do much to fix *It* if you think someone or something else will fix it for you. Suppose you're the boss. Which would you rather hear from a product development team: "Hey, boss, we've got a big problem here" or "We see a problem here and have several thoughts about how to go about solving it"? Of course, you'd rather hear the latter.

> *Total Ownership requires agreement and*
> *involvement with respect to Key Results.*

As with accountability, people talk a lot about ownership these days, but most cannot give you a clear, concise definition of what it actually means. If you look it up in the dictionary, you will find that most definitions of ownership have to do with rights to govern or control. But for us, taking the Own It step goes way beyond a dictionary's definition of ownership. In our experience, someone demonstrates ownership when they are able to connect present circumstances with both the past and the future. More specifically, ownership is the ability to make a connection between where you are today and what you have either done or failed to do in the past that put you in your current circumstances. All of us have made decisions, taken actions, and responded to information that has led us to our current circumstances. We need to own those realities. When we do own them, we find greater power to affect our futures. With this deeper understanding of what it means to Own It, we can more quickly make the connection between where we are today and where we want to be in the future, including what we will need to do in the present to ensure we get there.

Ownership means getting everyone out of the bleacher seats and onto the playing field, where they roll up their sleeves, go to work, and don't stop until they accomplish something that needs to be done. People who Own It are always actively involved. They take the needed actions, make the right things happen, and deliver the Key Results, regardless of whether they agree or disagree with the need or rationale for obtaining those results.

Can You Make the Connection?

A few years ago, we began an engagement with the fastest-growing health insurance company in the United States. The company had missed plan two years in a row, and it was looking like the company would fail to deliver again this year. One of the company's Key Results was "a successful January first." A successful January first meant that on January first, everyone who was covered by the company for medical insurance had their coverage in the system and ready to go by the first day of the year. Several of the company's key leaders had reached out to PIL for help to get this Key Result back on track.

Our preparations for the first meeting made it clear that we were walking into a highly charged situation with strong personalities and passionate leaders, who cared deeply about the business. We started the meeting by facilitating a discussion between the sales and operations leaders. Unfortunately, the first meeting quickly devolved into a classic illustration of the blame game. The longtime head of operations took great pains not to seem combative. But it was obvious that he was beyond frustrated with the sales team. He was cautious in his delivery but clear in his message: The sales team was at fault for being behind on January first. The sales leader, on the other hand, made her feelings equally clear. "I don't even want to be at this meeting. These meetings with consultants are a total waste of time. We just need operations to fix the problem."

We found the predicament fascinating and predictable. Each team actually took ownership for their own team's deliverables, but neither of them was taking ownership for the overall company Key Result of a successful January first. That single disconnect resulted in an extremely dysfunctional working relationship between the two teams. We see this happen frequently at the beginning of working relationships with clients. Operations was focused and working tirelessly to "lean out" their process for continuous improvement. Sales was busy focusing on their well-oiled selling system for ensuring that sales reps hit their numbers. But neither of these teams had sufficiently yoked their respective processes and systems to collaboratively hit the company's Key Result of a successful January first. Preoccupied with mowing their own piece of the turf, neither could see or own the need to keep the entire field in peak playing condition. As a result, the overall company was underperforming.

As the meeting continued, operations blamed sales for giving its people late information, forcing them to adjust their normal processes and take shortcuts that led to delays that, in turn, robbed other projects of sorely needed resources. Overtime costs were going through the roof. Sales complained that operations was making everything overly complex by wrapping its processes in a lot of useless red tape that made decision making difficult. "Operations wants so many reports and ongoing data evaluations that we spend more time documenting sales than closing sales."

By midmorning of the daylong meeting, we felt the timing was right to give the operations and sales teams some very pointed advice: "You both need to get Above the Line to See It more and Own It more." Fortunately, it didn't take long for them to respond accountably to our feedback. Within minutes we sensed a shift in the tone and tenor of the meeting. Members of the operations team acknowledged that they needed to be more aggressive and effective in simplifying their processes and letting go of some of their required reports. Members of the sales team also chimed in, admitting that they could do a better job getting operations the customer information it needed in a timelier fashion.

Above the Line: Once you See It, you can choose to Own It.

As both teams began to take ownership for the company's overall situation, you could feel the icy tension in the room melt. Both teams began working on what else they could do to achieve a successful January first for the company. The rest is history. The organization closed its gaps and delivered its most successful January first in recent memory. In full transparency, both operations and sales openly acknowledged that their teams still had work to do to improve collaboration and coordination, but both teams were proud that they had sustained a higher level of collaborative performance ever since they began working Above the Line to deliver the company's Key Results.

Own It Principles

Over the past thirty years we have studied and documented the indispensable role that ownership plays in achieving individual, team, and organizational results. To help our clients better understand the relationship between ownership and results, we developed a model that provides an easy-to-remember snapshot of the most common Levels of Ownership:

Four Levels of Ownership

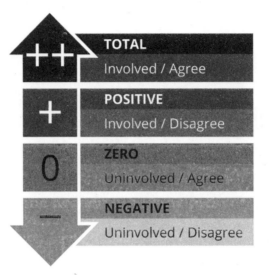

Note the two key elements that determine each level of ownership: Agreement and Involvement. As you consider each of the Levels of Ownership in more detail, pay close attention to these key elements. Not surprisingly, Total Ownership resides at the top, but for the purpose of highlighting the movement from bottom to top, we're going to start at the bottom to help you gain greater appreciation for the two highest levels of ownership.

1. Understand the Consequences of (–) Negative Ownership.
2. Resist the Deception of (0) Zero Ownership.

3. Embrace the Advantage of (+) Positive Ownership.
4. Harvest the Power of (++) Total Ownership.

To bring the Levels of Ownership to life, consider this major transformation undertaken by a client, one of the largest casual dining restaurants in the world. Their executive team had become increasingly concerned about a challenging shift in consumer preferences relative to quick-service dining options, made popular by competitors such as Chipotle. In the Chipotle model customers found simple menus, quality food, and good service that was as fast as that of virtually any fast-food option. In addition to this shift in consumer preferences, the CEO and senior leadership team were experiencing pressure from the board to improve the company's bottom line. The fix for both of these challenges was to introduce a highly simplified menu, shrinking from 139 items to 74 items.

1. Understand the Consequences of (−) Negative Ownership

As the new revised menu launched, senior field leaders immediately noticed general managers in the stores responding to the menu changes with different levels of ownership. A small yet vocal group ended up disagreeing with the menu change and was completely uninvolved in making the effort successful. The following comments coming up through the ranks were heard daily: "No one bothered to ask me about what menu items my customers wanted to see in this update. You won't find me supporting it. Corporate will pay the price they deserve on this one."

Negative Ownership = Uninvolved and Disagree

Individuals who don't agree with a leader's direction and spend most of their time sowing the seeds of misalignment, disagreement, resentment, and dysfunction among the larger team pull the organization backward. This (–) Negative Ownership posture, where people *disagree* with the direction and refuse to get *involved* in its implementation and achievement, undermines the delivery of Key Results at every turn. Issues and problems remain unseen and unaddressed as people purposefully withhold information needed to identify, correct, and resolve them. Additionally, individuals at the (–) Negative Ownership level rarely remain quiet about their discontent. They often work to recruit allies to support their disgruntled positions, often becoming a cancer that infects the entire culture. If and when management invites the infected individuals to leave the organization, colleagues often lament that it took them too long to do so, allowing needless damage to occur. When you add up their lack of agreement and their lack of involvement, you get (–) Negative Ownership that actually pulls you backward. Calculating the cost of permitting even a small percentage of their managers to remain at (–) Negative Ownership motivated senior leaders to work diligently to get these managers involved.

2. Resist the Deception of (0) Zero Ownership

But (–) Negative Ownership was not their only problem. Within restaurant operations, district managers also found store general managers who demonstrated (0) Zero Ownership. "Yes, I *agree* we need to simplify our menu. That change has been a long time coming. But our success in the restaurant is entirely dependent on whether marketing makes the right decisions. I hope they can figure this out before creating too much angst with our customer base. We'll just need to wait and see."

Zero Ownership = Uninvolved and Agree

This sort of attitude reflects agreement with the need to change the menu but no intent to be involved in its successful implementation. Basically, a leader with (0) Zero Ownership has thoughts like these: "I agree something needs to be done, but it's not my job to figure this out. It's *their* problem. Let *them* figure it out." The problem here is, people really believe it's not their job to be involved. For this reason, (0) Zero Ownership can be very *deceptive*. On the surface it sounds like there is some ownership. People speak to the issue at hand with passion, fully acknowledging the severity of the situation. They nod their heads in agreement that a problem needs to be solved or that an outcome needs to be achieved but then exempt themselves from actually participating in the process of solving it or engaging with the team to achieve it. If left alone, (0) Zero Ownership can establish a precedent for inaction throughout the organization. For those at (0) Zero Ownership, the buck keeps passing without ever landing on anyone's desk. Yes, these individuals positively See It, and even nod their heads as they hear others discuss the need to Own It, but they remain uninvolved and make no effort to Solve It, becoming part of the problem themselves and impeding the overall capacity of the organization to Do It. Again, the cost to our client of permitting even a small percentage of their managers to remain at (0) Zero Ownership motivated senior leaders to work diligently to get these managers involved.

3. Embrace the Advantage of (+) Positive Ownership

This brings us to (+) Positive Ownership: those who disagree with the target but are entirely involved in achieving it. Their disagreement can manifest itself in countless ways. Some may disagree because the metric and target they've been asked to deliver don't seem reasonable. Others might disagree simply because they lack data or understanding or needed context. Still others could decide, based on their own criteria, that they can't understand the decision and argue for a change in direction. So, what's the advantage of (+) Positive Ownership? It's simple: While people with (+) Positive Ownership openly communicate their disagreement, they are committed to focusing on what else they can do to get the needed result and taking the necessary actions to make it happen. In this case, their involvement speaks louder than their disagreement.

Positive Ownership = Involved and Disagree

Beyond the restaurant chain's more than two thousand district and general managers, there were many associates in the stores who didn't agree with the changes to the menu. Some of these associates were upset that their customers' buying habits weren't given more weight during the decision-making process. They freely shared their belief that their customers wouldn't make the transition with impunity. They further wondered about the analysis that was used to back this decision because sales had been up for two straight years. But what made both managers and associates at the (+) Positive Ownership level unique is that in spite of their disagreement, they moved forward and took accountability for their involvement in successfully implementing the menu and engaging their fellow associates to do the same.

(+) Positive Ownership propels you forward precisely because people at this level take positive steps, despite the fact that they disagree. We have seen many leaders make unpopular decisions and still lead people to be actively involved in achieving the desired outcomes. Consider for a moment your own Above the Line responses to direction or decisions with which you did not necessarily agree. Were you able to get past your disagreement and focus your attention on getting the result? If you were, you were at (+) Positive Ownership. If you were not able to move past your disagreement and get involved in achieving the result, you were at (–) Negative Ownership.

In terms of the Levels of Ownership, both leaders and individuals remain Below the Line until they reach the (+) Positive Ownership level, where people are entirely involved in achieving the result, in spite of their disagreement. So, what's the real difference between (–) Negative Ownership and (+) Positive Ownership? Look again at the Levels of Ownership model. People at both (+) Positive and

(–) Negative Levels of Ownership disagree with either the decision or the direction. There is no difference there. What's different is their level of involvement. With (–) Negative Ownership, people remain entirely uninvolved in achieving the needed outcome or advancing the particular decision. With (+) Positive Ownership, people are involved, deliberately focusing their actions on doing what it takes to deliver the result or move things forward.

We remember working with Randy Tobias, CEO of Eli Lilly, after he left his position at AT&T. He wasn't at Lilly very long before he boldly stated that he could not find even one person at the company who was accountable for any single decision. At Eli Lilly the culture was 100 percent consensus driven. We were with Randy when he confronted his leadership team, declaring, "Teams don't make decisions, leaders do. Teams help leaders make the right decision." There is great learning here. Leaders are accountable to make decisions and lead their teams forward to achieve results. They don't always have the time to get everyone on their teams or throughout their organizations to agree with their decisions and direction. The advantage of (+) Positive Ownership is something every leader should experience and embrace. It is the propelling advantage of working with people to move past their disagreement, align with direction, and take accountability to get involved and achieve desired outcomes. (+) Positive Ownership is an advantage in every organization and for every leader who can motivate people to act, despite their disagreement.

4. Harvest the Power of (++) Total Ownership

Finally, we come to (++) Total Ownership, where people fully agree with and quickly become involved in delivering the needed direction, target, or outcome. Their agreement and buy-in are what separate them from the (+) Positive Level of Ownership. Because of their agreement they do not, even for a moment, vacillate between opinions. Once a decision is made they move without hesitation and immediately invest themselves in delivering the targeted result. They bring their best creative selves to their jobs, never giving up, always rejecting Below the Line thinking, and working tirelessly to succeed. (++) Total Ownership is where people both agree with the decision or direction and are involved in achieving the desired outcomes. When it comes to the Key Results, senior leaders must "Plus Up" their ownership and buy in to the Key Results by becoming personally invested in achieving them. For leaders of the senior-most levels there is no room for disagreement on the Key Results if you want to accelerate and propel your organization forward.

Total Ownership = Involved and Agree

The CEO of this global restaurant group turned to his leadership team and defined his expectation: "We cannot go forward with this change in strategy without Total Ownership from every member of this team. It's time to 'Plus Up' our ownership, have the discussion and debate we need to resolve any and all concerns, and gain agreement on our Key Results and our strategy to achieve them. We cannot afford to have any disagreement on these Key

Results in this room. Let's have the discussion we need and then let's go forward together to implement our strategy with perfect alignment around what we are trying to achieve. What questions do we need to answer so we can move forward with (++) Total Ownership of our Key Results?"

Because everyone on the senior leadership team was willing to Plus Up, agreeing on the Key Results and strategy while being 100 percent invested and involved in their achievement, people at every management level right down to the store general managers moved quickly to higher levels of ownership. Immediate course corrections were made. Powerful stories were deliberately and frequently told about how the new menu allowed for better up-sale conversations with guests. Data was free flowing, showing the efficiencies that occurred in the kitchen due to menu simplification. Food was getting to the table hotter and faster. After successfully implementing its new strategy, the restaurant chain posted record sales numbers within the first six months and delivered one of the best years ever, allowing more profits than the board had requested to hit the company's bottom line.

Link Own It to Key Results

Our extensive workplace accountability study reveals that an alarming number of employees do their daily work at either the Zero or Positive levels of ownership. Further investigation reveals that they do so because they don't understand the "why" behind the Key Results (*agreement*) and/or they can't connect what they do every day to having an impact on the Key Results (*involvement*). If you want to create greater ownership, you must think of involvement and agreement as equally yoked and critically vital.

Total Ownership depends on people embracing the fact that their work directly or indirectly impacts the Key Results. It's important to reinforce that a lack of agreement can take many different forms—many of them rational and even compelling in nature. Whatever form disagreement takes, it almost always indicates that those disagreeing do not have the information, understanding, or strategic context they need to reach the level of Total Ownership.

One of our colleagues, Brad Starr, tells a story that nicely illustrates this point. On a business trip, he found himself assigned to a seat in one of the two exit rows of an airplane about to roll onto the runway. As the plane's engines roared to life, the flight attendant launched into her prepared preflight exit-row briefing. Glancing around, Brad saw that his companions were chatting, watching movies, reading books, using their phones to text and check emails, or posting on social media, not paying one iota of attention to the attendant's safety speech. The attendant, clearly perturbed by the passengers' apathy, departed from her usual script and said something that made everyone perk up their ears: "In my eighteen years of flying, there've been only two times when the plane I was on has filled with smoke and we had to get everyone out."

She now had everyone's attention. "One of those occasions went badly; the other went pretty well. The bad experience happened because the person sitting in that window seat right there pulled the door off, dropped it in the aisle, and instead of staying to help other people, jumped out and onto the slide. The rocking concave door was stopping others from getting out. It was a mess! People were tripping and falling, while black smoke was filling up the cabin. It turned into a stampede when we had to send everybody to other exits. The time everything went really well the passengers had actually *listened* to my instructions. I don't expect that to happen on this flight, but I need to know if *you* know how to help us get off this plane if it does." As Brad recalled later, "It was pretty amazing; it felt like people were suddenly taking notes! A piece of communication we'd half heard hundreds of times suddenly became compelling. What was so great about the incident was the attendant told us *why* her briefing was vital to our safety and *why* we needed to pay attention to it. She created immediate agreement and involvement."

Think about the four reactions to the restaurant's menu changes. The journey from Negative Ownership to Total Ownership follows a path from no understanding and no involvement to full awareness of why it's important and total involvement in making it happen. It reminds us of the old story about three bricklayers working on the foundation of a new building. When a passerby asked them what they were doing, the first bricklayer said he was laying bricks. The second bricklayer said he was putting up a wall. The third bricklayer said he was building a cathedral. They were all doing the same thing. The first had a job. The second had a career. The third had a cause.

Involvement does not come as easily. Consider the image that pops into your mind when you hear, "Maggie is totally *involved* in what she's doing." Most likely, you picture a woman putting every ounce of her focus, concentration, energy, and creativity into the task at hand, whether she's arranging flowers or piloting a fighter jet. Let's suppose she and her teammate Suman are members of a team selling hammers and screwdrivers. Their manager tells them, "Look, team, you need to sell a lot more screwdrivers right now because we get a much higher profit margin on screwdrivers." Suman agrees wholeheartedly, exclaiming, "Absolutely, boss, I totally get it. I'll sell a ton of screwdrivers." At the end of the week, he has sold 2,000 hammers and only 120 screwdrivers, because, it turns out, it's a heck of a lot easier to sell hammers than screwdrivers. He agreed, but he didn't get involved. As for Maggie, after she said, "You've got it, boss," she purposefully tweaked her normal sales calls to focus on the benefits of ordering screwdrivers right now. She came back at the end of the week having sold 1,000 hammers and 1,200 screwdrivers. You guessed it. She not only agreed, she got totally involved. Suman Saw It; Maggie Saw It and Owned It.

Perhaps Suman's boss did not make the goal clear enough. As we discussed in chapter 2, you must make Key Results perfectly clear to those who are accountable for achieving them.

As you create more agreement and more involvement, you'll see ownership rise dramatically in your teams and across your organization. Be purposeful in describing the "why" behind your requests. Help people make the link between their work and achieving the Key Results. At the end of the day, people want to know why they're going in a specific direction and that they are personally contributing to the team or organization actually getting there.

Getting Accountability Right:
Moving to Above the Line Ownership

1. A vice president of operations facilitated a discussion on how his team was impacting sales by managing inventory levels. Data from the sales team showed that when clients had to wait an extra three days for product, sales dropped by 44 percent. Once the operations team saw how its management of inventory impacted sales, every team member moved from Zero Ownership (Agree but Uninvolved) to Total Ownership (Agree and Involved). From then on, they all looked at inventory levels much more carefully and closely.

2. The CEO of the restaurant group mentioned earlier in this chapter recently provided his leadership team with updated sales targets and an invitation to get involved in visiting restaurants every week, regardless of their functional roles. In other words, he wanted support functions like HR and marketing to be in their restaurants as much as operational leaders, elevating their involvement in delivering the Key Results.

3. A CEO of a major hospital in Richmond, Virginia, models his "involvement" to each member of his executive team for their "Patient Experience" Key Result by participating in hourly rounding visits with patients every morning after coming to work.

4. A global quick service dining company had experienced significant food safety issues. Initial efforts to fix the food safety issues were viewed as heavy-handed and parental by much of the workforce. Setting up cameras within every restaurant, for

example, led many employees to feel Zero Ownership and a lack of trust from their senior leaders. We worked with their new chief operating officer to immediately target the disagreement with data from competitors who were leading the industry in food safety. That effort, coupled with aggressive interpretation around the desired beliefs that leadership wanted employees to hold about the cameras, led their organization on a steady climb toward embracing this important strategic shift.

Chapter Five

SOLVE IT

Obtaining the Wisdom to Solve What You Own

Highly accountable people put all their creative energy into delivering results, while people stuck Below the Line waste their energy concocting justifications for why they are not delivering results. As we have described in earlier chapters, this applies to individuals, teams, and entire organizations. Exceptional results are achieved by people who refuse to divert any of their their creative energy toward excuse making. Furthermore, exceptional results are achieved by people who always figure out what else they can do to succeed. When it comes to the Solve It step, high achievers channel their creative thinking into answering this deceptively simple, yet powerfully propelling question: "What else can I do?" Whenever they encounter problems that defy conventional solutions, they dig deeper and go outside the box by asking, "What else can I do to solve this problem?" If achieving needed results begins to seem increasingly unattainable, they again ask themselves if there's something else they can do to get things back on track and moving in the right direction. By constantly and rigorously asking the Solve It question, they avoid slipping into the victim cycle as they encounter and address obstacles on the road to success. Asked over and over again, this question, "What else can I do?" reflects the Solve It attitude and mind-set that most often differentiates those who win from those who lose. As simple as the question is, it propels individuals, teams, and organizations to do more thinking and acting Above the Line.

What Else Can I Do?

One of the most impressive and inspiring leaders we've interacted with over the years is Jill Ragsdale, senior vice president and chief people and culture officer for Sutter Health in Northern California. We first met Jill after she had left her post as chief human resources officer at the Mayo Clinic and returned for a second stint at Sutter Health. Jill's responsibilities at Sutter consisted of not only administering the human resources function for nearly sixty thousand employees spread throughout dozens of hospitals and hundreds of outpatient clinics but also orchestrating a successful organizational transformation.

Upon Jill's return to Sutter Health we worked with her to establish the Key Results for the people and culture function. Her top priority was to focus the HR team on delivering higher Patient Satisfaction Scores for their health care system. Her second priority was to attack a commonly held perception among many of the employed clinicians that "HR is not easy to work with." A common complaint was that the "busywork" requirements associated with HR inevitably pulled clinicians away from treating patients—the very thing they most wanted to do. Given Jill's innate "no-ego" approach to getting results, she had no difficulty seeing and owning the feedback. One spring morning in Sacramento, she invited her extended leadership team into a room and spent most of the day discussing one question: "What else can we do to make HR easy to work with?" By the end of the meeting Jill had completed a list of shifts they needed to make to change the perception that HR was not easy to work with and demanded too much "busywork." On the list was taking back some of the self-service HR items that had been previously pushed out to them. Self-service had been a big push to create efficiencies, so this was a new idea to have HR take the work back to make things easier for managers. Examples included having HR complete the personnel change forms and handle requirement screening. As Jill and her team continued their quest to make HR easier to work with, the question "What else can we do?" enlivened and elevated the mind-set of the entire HR organization. Jill and her team eventually achieved appreciation and accolades from many clinicians, who came to see the HR organization as a united team committed to making their work lives more "patient centered." While it's fair to say that their intense focus on their patient satisfaction Key Result drove these efforts, the question "What else can we do?" was the actual catalyst for change.

Every leader, team, and organization wrestles from time to time with pesky problems that stand in the way of significant performance gains. But wasting time Below the Line by giving in to challenging circumstances will only dull your senses and diminish your imagination at the very time you most need to discover creative solutions. Not long ago we worked with the credit card division of one of the largest banks in the world. The senior executives at the credit card division wanted us to help them create greater accountability and ownership at every level of the division, particularly at the front line. The introduction of our methodologies was going smoothly when one of the regional vice presidents shared with us his deep concern about the poor performance and high turnover rate of a particular call center in his region. Simply put, customers who called the center to order a credit card often hung up during extended wait times and ended up getting a card from a competitor. The senior leadership team calculated that every extra second their customers had to wait translated into a million dollars of lost profits annually. With this reality in mind, the call center's management team set their sights on a major Key Result: reducing the average customer-response time by a whopping 50 percent, a huge challenge for a call center that had for years improved at no more than a snail's pace.

The several hundred employees in the call center quickly agreed on the importance of hitting this lofty target, but when it came to figuring out how to do it, they just scratched their heads and waited for something good to happen. They could See It, they even agreed to Own It, but they couldn't see the path to Solve It. It wasn't that they were unwilling; they were simply unable to unleash the creative thinking they needed to Solve It.

It's not that you can't Solve It, it's that you won't Solve It.

Once we drove home this point, the call center staff accepted the challenge and finally began to unlock their best thinking on what could be done differently to reduce call wait time. As they began more seriously asking, "What else can we do?" again and again, potential solutions began to emerge from the team, leading to deeper discussions that produced a growing list of potential solutions. Eventually, the proverbial light at the end of the tunnel began to shine.

Within a few weeks they began training everyone on the "swift and complete customer satisfaction" skills they expected current and new employees to display. New customer relationship management (CRM) software was acquired and installed. A simplified balanced scorecard was developed and implemented for measuring and reporting performance on a daily basis. The Solve It mentality flourished as new ideas for reducing the time needed to handle a call poured in from all directions. To this day the call center leaders and managers involved light up when they talk about the day the credit card division reported that the call center's performance improvements had added $143 million to the bottom line.

Creative thinking and innovative problem solving go viral when people take this third step to accountability seriously. That's when everyone begins contributing their best thinking to the cause. One leader told us jokingly, "We used to have a hard time coming up with new ideas. Now we get more than we can possibly handle!" Of course, not all solutions are good solutions, but even bad solutions can stimulate thinking that leads to better ones.

Do you remember the now famous statement made by Jim Lovell from Apollo 13? "Houston, we have a problem." Minutes later, he discovered that the spacecraft was venting a gas, which turned out to be the Command Module's oxygen. The Apollo 13 story beautifully illustrates the power of Solve It. From the moment the spacecraft suffered its crippling malfunction to the moment three

American astronauts landed safely in the water, the support team at NASA continued coming up with ingenious solutions to what seemed like unsolvable problems. At a crucial life-or-death moment when the CO_2 filters in the Command Module *Odyssey* failed, threatening the crew with suffocation, someone suggested replacing the failed filters with those designed for the Lunar Module. When that proved infeasible because one filter was round and the other one square, one of the NASA scientists focused entirely on finding a solution. He dumped all the items available to the astronauts on a table and said, pointing to the objects, "We have to make *this* filter fit with *that* filter with nothing but *that*." Fueled by their Total Ownership of the situation and their unified mission to bring the three astronauts back safely, the support team diligently sought solution after solution to overcome one problem after another. When all three astronauts returned safely, the Apollo 13 mission became known as the Successful Failure.

Solve It Principles

Four Solve It principles will help you stimulate the creative thinking needed to achieve Key Results:

1. Create Space for Others to Fill.
2. Engage More Brains at Work.
3. Stay Engaged, Be Persistent, Think Differently, and Create New Connections.
4. Maintain a Culture Intent on Achieving Key Results.

Let's examine these principles more closely.

1. Create Space for Others to Fill

Virtually every study of human capital that has examined the reasons behind employee turnover has found that most people leave their job because of their boss. Ask someone to describe the most effective leader they've worked for during their career and they will typically respond with adjectives such as *open, accessible, encouraging, collaborative, interested, supportive, kind, humble, available,* and *curious.* If you then ask about the worst boss, you'll hear the opposite descriptions. Nearly every desirable leadership skill links closely to openness, authenticity, and humility. Self-effacing, unpretentious leaders tend to display a high degree of empathy and emotional intelligence. They don't coerce and compel performance with a "tell 'em, bribe 'em, force 'em" approach to management. They're not so consumed by personal ambitions that they fail to listen to or learn from others. On the positive side, effective leaders know how to facilitate dialogue, create alignment, and move teams forward. They always know that they don't have all the answers, acknowledging that solutions to the most difficult problems lie beyond their own intellect and in the collective minds of their people. In short, they think and act in ways that engender Above the Line attitudes and mind-sets.

Applying the Solve It step requires openness, authenticity, and humility on the part of the leader. Inviting people to ask "What else can we do?" suggests that the leader expects them to come up with the best answers. Arrogant, egoistical, and overconfident leaders will often think to themselves, "What else can I do to show people my awesome power?" Hey, look, it's a superhero! What a beautiful cape, what a guy, what a gal! But look again, and you will see someone who easily falls prey to the Emperor's New Clothes syndrome, gaining the verbal admiration of people while failing to win their minds and hearts.

The superhero syndrome usually surfaces when managers rely on the antiquated command-and-control "tell 'em what to do" approach to the job. Managers cut from this mold will find applying the Solve It step particularly challenging. In one of our recent client interviews, a front-line worker shared the following: "My boss believes that managers should manage and that hourly workers should do what they're told. The trouble is, most of our workers are perfectly happy with that arrangement. They want generous wages and benefits, of course, but they do not want to take responsibility for anything more than doing their own jobs the way they have always done them." This weak and limiting mind-set arises when the leader constantly straps on the cape, swoops into a troubled situation, "solves the problem," and then swoops out. Ironically, leaders who believe they can create accountability this way end up ensuring a lack of accountability. "It's not our job to be creative problem solvers. The boss will do it for us."

If you've ever helped a child who is struggling with a difficult math problem, you know that it's not helpful in the long run to remove that burden by saying, "Wow. This homework is pretty tough. Why don't you run outside and play? I'll do it for you." Intuitive parents understand that the struggle itself fuels growth and ownership. They encourage the learner by asking such questions as "How else could you look at this? Can you think of another approach that might work?" Effective leaders do the same. They resist the temptation to jump in and Solve It themselves and instead maximize the human capital entrusted to their leadership by encouraging everyone to keep asking, "What else can I do?"

For years we've invited senior leaders in both large and small organizations to describe the central purpose of leadership. They typically say the following:

- Create vision.
- Execute on strategic direction.
- Get people aligned and moving together.
- Facilitate the removal of obstacles that are standing in the way of those who do the work.

While each of these answers makes sense and is important in and of itself, we prefer to say that the primary job of a leader is to get people to think and act in ways that will help them achieve the Key Results. The most effective leaders we've seen create ample space for their people to take accountability for doing whatever it takes to make sure the organization thrives in this fiercely competitive, fast-changing world. They foster productive *thinking.* They make it clear that they value creativity and innovation. They facilitate movement in the needed direction by stimulating people to do something else, something different, to achieve Key Results.

Successful implementation of the Solve It step depends on leaders who acknowledge that the best thinking almost always comes from those closest to the actual work. A good example comes from a client we've worked with over the years—the Domino's organization. Founded in 1960, Domino's Pizza eventually became the recognized world leader in pizza delivery, operating a network of company-owned and franchise-owned stores in the United States and abroad. The company's success stemmed, in large part, from the fact that Domino's leaders assembled a group of exceptional people to pursue a mission to become the best pizza delivery company in the world. That was not always the case. At one point Wall Street and market analysts were hammering the company for lackluster performance. To help turn around that dismal performance, Domino's engaged Partners In Leadership to work with more than three hundred top leaders at the company's national sales meeting.

It was a precarious time in their history. They needed to identify the reasons behind recent performance gaps and implement a positive approach to creating greater accountability for doing better. Internationally, no one could compete with them. But, domestically, they were losing market share fast to Pizza Hut, Little Caesars, and Papa John's. During the meeting with the top three hundred leaders, Dave Brandon, their CEO, made two major points in his opening remarks. First, he notified the group that for the first time in decades, they would not be receiving bonuses. Second, he told them that they could not keep excusing poor performance by blaming the loss of market share on the new five-dollar pizza competitors. "We are *not* the five-dollar pizza company. Pizza Hut and Papa John's are our competitors, *not* Little Caesars. We're better than that. We make a better pizza than that!"

Then he introduced us. After we explained our process for

instilling greater accountability for achieving results throughout the company we stepped down from the stage and walked over to join a conversation between Dave Brandon and his VP of international sales, Pat Doyle. We listened as Pat respectfully asked Dave, "Why *can't* we compete in that space? If there's market share to be had, we're good enough to rescale and go after that business." Dave, to his credit, checked his ego and thoughtfully responded, "Well, let's talk further about that."

When Dave finally approved the idea, Pat began working on ways to penetrate the affordable pizza niche. Three months later, Domino's launched a national ad campaign with Dave Brandon himself pitching their five-dollar pizza. In the ad, he promised that Domino's was not going to bail out Mr. and Mrs. Wall Street but rather Mr. and Mrs. Main Street. He donned a delivery vest, grabbed some pizzas, jumped into a Prius, and drove off to deliver on Domino's five-dollar pizza campaign. The tactic sparked a huge turnaround for the company.

Dave turned out to be a pretty good actor, but when it came to making a great-tasting five-dollar pizza, it all depended on the cooks in the kitchen who kept asking "What else can I do?" until they got the new recipe right. Some of the veteran cooks had been involved in creating the original recipe years earlier. They found it hard to check their ego at the door and admit that they could do better, but that did not stop them from striving to find the best solutions to Domino's problem. They didn't do it because Dave ordered them to do it. They did it because they took accountability for attaining the company's Key Results.

In its ongoing effort to Solve It, Domino's would soon launch a new ad campaign that broke the rules of traditional marketing. In a new ad, it showed real customers complaining that Domino's pizza "tasted like cardboard." The commercial showed Domino's senior leaders agreeing with that opinion and admitting they needed to make it tastier. "We hear you. We'll bring you something better. If you don't love it, we'll give you your money back." Wow! Talk about putting your money where your mouth is!

Domino's ego-free attack on the problem, its acknowledgment that the company had for too long ignored its customers' voices, and its willingness to change the recipe on which it had built its former success propelled the company to massive profits. Domino's would go on to perform the most significant turnaround in fast-food industry history. Over an eight-year span between 2010 and 2018 Domino's stock moved from $3 a share to nearly $300 a share, outperforming even Netflix, Tesla, and Amazon over the same time frame. Their culture and results have been thriving Above the Line.

2. Engage More Brains at Work

Repeatedly asking the question "What else can I do?" helps stimulate the higher levels of involvement we recommended in chapter 4. It reinforces ownership among those already involved and invites the uninvolved to get more involved. When that happens, a Culture of Accountability begins to take hold.

Pixar offers a great case in point. Ed Catmull, cofounder of Pixar Animation Studios and president of Pixar Animation and Disney Animation, once disclosed in an interview: "At Pixar, we believe strongly that filmmakers should develop ideas they are passionate about. This may sound like a no-brainer, but in fact, the big movie studios in Hollywood have whole departments devoted to acquiring and developing projects that will only later be paired with a director for hire. Pixar, by contrast, never buys pitches from the outside. Instead, we encourage our people to build their ideas from scratch and we give them the resources and, crucially, the candid feedback that are required to transform the first wisps of a story into a truly compelling film."

By emphasizing the behavior inherent in the Solve It step, Pixar produced an unprecedented string of hit movies. Pixar's people solve the problem every filmmaker faces: the need for fresh and audience-pleasing ideas. Most important, those who come up with the best ideas at Pixar can see them through to completion. We love the Pixar story because it illustrates an understanding of the basic human desire to create something. Human beings come hardwired with that desire. We want to create or improve things. We seek to build a career, establish a home, start and raise a family. We involve ourselves in creating and improving the life that surrounds us. Leaders who invite everyone in their organization to solve and improve the world around them reap the benefits of their people's innate desire to contribute value to that world.

We think Catmull would agree. He once said, "The Braintrust, a group of smart, passionate people, meets every few months or so to assess each movie we're making. It helps identify and solve whatever problems are keeping the film from working, not by prescribing the answer but by breaking down whatever flaws exist and spitballing various fixes. Notably, in the wake of a Braintrust meeting, it is up to the director to figure out precisely how to remedy the problems. The Braintrust merely helps tease out the errors in logic or focus. But it only works if you create and protect a culture of candor at your company in which anyone can communicate with anyone else without fear of reprisal."

In that spirit, Partners In Leadership has developed a digital crowdsourcing app called *Propeller* to help our clients engage in virtual conversations about topics that matter most to their organization. It enables leaders to pose a question to a large group of employees, inviting everyone to chime in with solutions, debate ideas, and vote the best ideas to the top of the list. When, for example, a leader poses a question about ways to reduce the organization's cost structure, that question will prompt hundreds or even thousands of people to post ideas and comments within hours. As the process unfolds, the best thinking percolates its way to the top.

By asking the Solve It question digitally, leaders also create conversations with millennials in a channel of communication that generation loves. Oh, and there's a terrific side effect: Leaders who use these types of tools dramatically reduce the need for meetings, thereby saving the countless hours spent in an activity most people dread.

3. Stay Engaged, Be Persistent, Think Differently, and Create New Connections

Every road to Key Results hits snags and bumps and potholes and detours along the way. We'd like to offer a few tips on overcoming those inevitable obstacles:

Stay Engaged. Often, when a problem persists, people naturally feel tempted to give up, to slip Below the Line to wait and see if things will get better on their own. As you implement the Solve It step, avoid this trap by staying engaged in the process of finding solutions and assuming full accountability for discovering solutions that will ultimately deliver desired results. Such solutions generally come only when you take the initiative to explore, search, and question, even after you think you have done everything you can. Understanding that others may not share the same level of ownership or desire to achieve a goal, you must take the initiative yourself. Which would you rather be: someone who watches things happen, someone who wonders what happened, someone who never knew anything happened, or someone who *makes* things happen?

Be Persistent. You must constantly ask the Solve It question: "What else can I do?" Repetition makes posing the question an ingrained habit. It makes it possible for you to keep formulating the creative solutions that propel progress. As a capable and inspired leader once told us, "That which we persist in doing becomes easier for us to do; not that the nature of the thing itself is changed but that our power to *do* is increased."

Think Differently. Albert Einstein once said, "The significant problems we face cannot be solved at the same level of thinking we were at when we created them." In other words, the same thinking that got you into the problem won't get you out of it. Always solicit and strive to understand a wide range of different, even diametrically opposed, perspectives. Never focus on what can't be done or what you can't control. Keep searching. Remember that looking for "what else" often means looking for something different.

Create New Connections. Many solutions require innovative approaches that tap into unfamiliar ways of thinking about a problem. You can take advantage of new perspectives by forging relationships with people you may not have previously considered as sources of good ideas. Previously unconsidered relationships may include your competitors, your suppliers and vendors, or someone in another department in the company. Tom Smith and Craig Hickman remind us that early on in their writing of *The Oz Principle* they were struggling with what to name the book. Their literary agent, Michael Snell, was out at dinner with his wife, Pat, and asked her what she thought about when considering the victim mind-set of those who live, act, and work Below the Line and those who take the Steps to Accountability. She immediately stated, "Oh, that's just like Dorothy and her companions on the Yellow Brick Road!" The next day Michael called Tom and Craig to see what they could do with the Wizard of Oz. It resonated immediately! Their very first thought was that half of corporate America was off to see the wizard, or in other words, they were looking externally, outside themselves, for someone or something to give them the needed answers to overcome their problems. They, like Dorothy and her companions, were off to see the wizard! After exploring this idea further, they landed on the name for the book: *The Oz Principle.*

4. Maintain a Culture Intent on Achieving Key Results

Nothing empowers an organization to achieve Key Results more than creating a Culture of Accountability in which people take accountability to think and act in the manner necessary to achieve results. It's so important that Tom published an entire book on the subject: *Change the Culture, Change the Game.* You may recall the point made in chapter 1 that accountability spreads and sticks in an organization when people use a common framework and language to talk about it. In chapter 9 we will show you how to build and maintain an Above the Line Culture, but for now just keep in mind that it takes more than a great leader and a few brilliant problem solvers to make a good company great.

Our Workplace Accountability Study suggests that when it comes to habitually asking "What else can I do?" most teams rank themselves around 5.5 on a 10-point scale. When probed for an explanation, people answer in a couple different ways. Some suggest, "We just don't have time to go through all of that every time a snowball hits the fan." From our experience, we would counter with what we have observed: Those who don't take the time to Solve It end up getting buried under an avalanche of problems. Ironically, some people interpret the Solve It question as "What *more* can I do?" which is not the same as "What *else* can I do?" There's a huge difference between the two. "More" can mean "more of the same old, same old." It's not just about doing more! The word *else* suggests coming up with something new, different. "More" often courts failure; "else" generates creative new thinking that leads to success.

Most students of business history admire the way Toyota has changed the entire world of manufacturing by applying its own version of the Solve It question. According to a *Fortune* magazine article, "Toyota is big, famously conservative, and hugely successful. Why mess with a good thing? In fact, the company that the Massachusetts Institute of Technology report 'The Machine That

Changed the World' called the most efficient automaker anywhere is rethinking almost everything it does. Turning Japan's unnerving stubborn economic slump into an opportunity, Toyota is reorganizing its operations, putting still more high technology into its factories, and reworking its legendary 'lean production' system. Even if some of the measures fail, Toyota is likely to emerge an even more vigorous global competitor." Not overreacting when profits begin to decline, the company continues to encourage its entire workforce to seek new solutions. As a prime example of a Solve It company, Toyota thrives on challenges, always searching for ways to do things better and remaining agile and flexible in every nook and cranny of the organization. Donald N. Smith, a manufacturing expert at the University of Michigan's engineering school and a longtime Toyota watcher, warns Toyota's competitors to keep a watchful eye on the company that has demonstrated the capacity to continually improve itself with an undying and unwavering Solve It culture that will most likely ensure its standout performance for years to come.

Getting Accountability Right: Solving It by Asking, "What Else Can I Do?"

1. One of our retail clients needed to figure out ways to get new products sold more quickly. We put every one of the company's top four hundred leaders in the room and organized them into groups of five. Then we asked each group to come up with as many solutions to the problem as they could in ten minutes. We gave them only two constraints: The solution can't require more resources or budget and it can't require approval from

further up the organizational hierarchy. After ten minutes, each group produced an average of seventeen solutions. Next, we asked each group to identify their top two solutions. Four months later they had already seen $4 million in new revenue come from those solutions.

2. More health-care organizations are establishing senior-level teams that are dedicated to asking, "What else can we do to strategically position our organization for growth in the future?" The entire purpose of these teams is to think innovatively about the way they offer care to their consumer base in the years ahead.

3. Many teams within our clients' organizations have begun using virtual Solve It exercises as a way to rethink and repurpose time spent in meetings. How many of you would like to have some time back on your calendar? Target a sixty-minute meeting on your calendar and, instead of meeting, ask everyone involved to spend fifteen minutes in a virtual Solve It exercise offering creative solutions to a problem in your organization. Not only will the solutions come fast and easy in a form that is easy to digest, everyone will get forty-five minutes back on their calendars! Download the *Propeller* app to get access to virtual Solve It exercises.

4. We have clients who create meaningful competitions and awards around the best ideas that are offered to move the needle on Key Results. One client in the consumer energy space created a Wall of Fame to highlight "Above the Line Solutions" that had been implemented in the company because of input offered by front-line employees.

Chapter Six

DO IT

Exercising the Will to Do What You See, Own, and Solve

When Friday's leadership meeting ended, the CEO of a large wire and cable manufacturing company asked his EVP of operations to pull together the company's most recent sales numbers. As chairs pushed away from the table and the leaders began leaving the room, the CEO realized he hadn't been clear about *when* he needed the data. He asked the EVP if he could hold on a minute.

"Just out of curiosity, when do you think I want that sales data?"

The EVP responded, "I'm going to set aside my overtime analysis project and work on it right away."

"Sorry, I wasn't clear. I don't need it until next Thursday. Keep plugging away on the overtime analysis. It's important."

"Got it, thanks."

Afterward, the CEO reminded himself that he needed to make the timetable perfectly clear when he asked someone to do something. Otherwise, he could inadvertently take someone off the path to Key Results. No matter what the task, you must always ask the key Do It question:

Who will do what by when?

Have you ever come to the end of a meeting and wondered exactly what you should do and by when? It happens a lot, especially when the person making a request is *unclear* about the importance or urgency of the task. When a senior leader asks for something, people tend to make it a top priority, although doing so may distract them from what they really need to do in order to make progress toward what matters most to the organization. "Who will do what by when?" keeps priorities straight by removing confusion and false assumptions about important tasks. In reality, if you can't answer the Do It question, "Who will do what by when?" you don't have a plan or a path forward.

Determine if the "who" is you.

To understand this principle, consider the following example for which we were fortunate enough to have a front row seat. Every production line in the company was running at a furious pace in order to keep up with the overwhelming global demand. And because the company's diagnostic products were responsible for saving lives every day, manufacturing mistakes on any production line were not an option. Here's how one of the company's production line managers helped achieve a manufacturing breakthrough and save millions of dollars as a result of boldly taking the step up from Solve It to Do It.

This particular production line manager clocked in at 7:30 a.m. every day with one thing on his mind: ensuring the line runs smoothly, without interruption, to produce the highest-quality diagnostic products on the market. On the day that began his breakthrough journey, he walked into an 8:00 a.m. meeting with the other production line managers at the plant. He scanned the crowded room, looking for an empty seat at the large table where colleagues are checking emails or chatting about their weekend plans. He was the last person to enter before the CEO arrived.

When the company's CEO entered the room, something that happened only occasionally, everyone turned off their phones, halted their conversations, and looked at her attentively. They were all a little apprehensive about this hastily scheduled leadership meeting with the CEO. It couldn't be good news.

Sure enough, the CEO got right to the point. "We have a time and materials waste problem and it's affecting our costs. We've got to contain costs if we're going to keep our products priced to sell. Otherwise, we're going to start losing customers. Let me be specific. We must eliminate another five million dollars in waste within the next eighteen months."

Since the manufacturing team had already internalized the Steps to Accountability, they quickly jumped into See It mode with this question: "What's the reality of our waste problem?"

After a robust discussion, the VP of operations summed things up by saying, "Well, we've done all of the easy and obvious things.

We've 'leaned out' our current process and have squeezed out as much waste as possible." Heads nodded. Then someone asked about the extent to which the team owned the problem. The plant controller raised his hand. "I think our ownership is quite high. We agree we need to slash more waste out of the plant and we're working on ways to do it. Actually, we've already come a long way."

Then, the production line manager who had entered the room just before the CEO spoke up. "That brings us to the next big question. What else can we do to Solve It? I've been lying awake at night thinking about this, and last night I thought of something pretty radical. What if we actually change our process? You know those glass beads we use in Phase Four of our manufacturing process? We always replace them with new beads every time we start a new run. What if we figured out a way to wash and sterilize the beads, then reuse them? It would save us hundreds of thousands of dollars that we currently spend on new beads."

This idea sparked some heated discussion. And although it struck everyone as an interesting idea, they decided that it was way too risky. They believed it was better to stay with a proven process than monkey with it and possibly wind up with a bigger problem.

The quality control VP summed up the consensus. "I'm not averse to taking risks, but this is one situation where it just doesn't make sense."

The CEO adjourned the meeting without any specific assignments. "Keep thinking. If we don't solve this waste problem, we could all be polishing our résumés next year."

As the production line manager who had offered the radical solution wandered back to his line, he felt increasingly frustrated by the meeting. He thought to himself, *Since when had the company's leadership team grown so afraid of their own shadow? If we can't take risks, we can't make the needed gains.* Sitting at his desk wrestling with his frustration, he looked up at the Steps to Accountability model taped to his wall. The Do It step lit up like a beacon. *Dang! We never even got to the Do It step. And what's more, we have a potential solution. Why don't I just go ahead and Do It?*

Grabbing a sharp pencil and a legal pad, the production line manager began sketching out a system that could scrub and sterilize the beads, then reuse them in the production process. The page soon looked like a nest of wires, but it was all very clear in his mind's eye. After a restless weekend, he came into the office two hours early on Monday morning and began setting up a small test line using beads from previous runs.

He and a few line operators carefully washed and sterilized the used beads, then tried running the line with them. The results looked promising. Over the next few days, additional test runs provided sufficient positive data to conduct a more precise analysis of the new process. Amazingly, it not only worked as well as the old process, it worked better. Somehow, the scrubbed beads could produce product faster than brand-new beads. It was a classic win-win. Scrubbing beads would not only save several hundred thousand dollars per year, but the more efficient production process would also reduce the time it took to complete a full production run.

After he showed his analysis to the CEO, she called another leadership meeting, at which the production line manager presented his findings and recommendation. The vote was unanimous. The CEO made it official. "We'll gradually introduce this to every production line in the plant." Within twelve months the company increased its production of defect-free medical diagnostic products on every production line, reducing costs well beyond the $5 million target.

What enabled the production line manager to Do It?

- He demonstrated the courage to do something despite the risk of failure. And he was willing to fail to find out if he might actually have a solution to the waste problem. It is often true that the faster we fail, the faster we succeed. Most of us don't come up with the perfect idea right out of the gate. Typically, the best ideas result from trying and trying and trying again. Sometimes the fifth time is the charm.
- He had internalized the Steps to Accountability and knew that solving it was not the endgame. He refused to fall back Below the Line after coming up with a viable solution. Since he knew that the CEO would not fire him for failing to pull off a new idea, he accepted the risks and stepped up to Do It. Remember what we said about individual and joint accountability? It's not that the job gets bigger, it's that we take accountability for something bigger than our job—achieving the Key Results!
- Sometimes it takes an entire team to make it happen; sometimes it takes just one person who despite the risks is unwilling to stop until the solution is found and implemented. Companies and teams achieve results when and only when they step up and Do It!

Do It Principles

Individuals, teams, and entire organizations slip Below the Line whenever they fail to carry out all four steps: See It, Own It, Solve It, and Do It. Unfortunately, there are many individuals, teams, and organizations that successfully Solve It and then fail to move forward and Do It. No matter how brilliantly you've traversed the first three steps, See It, Own It, and Solve It, they mean nothing unless you use them to Do It. The value of "ideation" manifests itself in the "doing."

These four Do It Principles will help you take that final step:

1. Learn from Failed Attempts to Do It.
2. Recognize That You're Not Taking Full Accountability Until You Do It.
3. Make the Do It Question Part of Every Meeting.
4. Never Stop Until You Achieve the Key Results.

Let's explore each one in detail.

1. Learn from Failed Attempts to Do It

Most people who fail to Do It find difficulty resisting the gravitational pull Below the Line, where they succumb to thinking like a victim and wasting valuable time, energy, and resources. In our experience, succumbing to such thinking happens because of a natural resistance to assuming the risks associated with taking decisive action. "What if I (we) fail?" A fear of failure can paralyze people. Of course, there are risks in moving forward and making mistakes, but there are also huge risks associated with standing still or perpetuating the status quo.

When it comes to following through on solutions, people tend to fall back Below the Line for two main reasons:

- An unwillingness to take the risks associated with action
- An inability to maintain the discipline it takes to keep going when the going gets tough

You must be willing to Do It, and you must commit yourself to doing it, no matter how many obstacles get in your way. Take Christy, for example. When the alarm clock clangs at 5:00 a.m., Christy opens her eyes and realizes she has roughly an hour before she needs to get the oldest of her five children out of bed and out the door. She feels so sleepy and cozy wrapped in her bed's warm blanket, so she rolls over and presses Snooze to silence the alarm. But she knows she has to get up and she does. If she doesn't, she won't possibly be able to do a five-mile run before the war of kids, showers, breakfast, shoes, backpacks, and bus stops begins. Why does she Do It? Because she knows that she needs to keep fit for herself and for her family.

Now take a look at her neighbor, Cindy, who also has five kids. Cindy also rolls over and punches the alarm clock, but she falls back to sleep. A few minutes later, her eyes fly open. She runs through the Steps to Accountability in her mind:

See It: "I know I've got to tie on my running shoes and do a quick few miles before I get the kids up. If I don't stay fit, they'll run me ragged."

Own It: "Nobody else is going to do it for me."

Solve It: "I'll hit the Snooze button one more time to get five more minutes of sleep, then I'll be ready to get up."

Do It: "I've already let ten minutes go by, so I'll just run more tomorrow to make up for missing today."

Cindy stays in bed for another hour, and when she does get up, she doesn't feel one bit more refreshed to meet the hectic day. She didn't get the result she wanted. She failed to see that accountability occurs only when you actually *follow through* and take the Do It step.

This happens constantly in teams and organizations everywhere. People sit in the bleacher seats as observers, keenly aware of the problems the participants on the field must confront to get results (See It), fully dedicated to the need for total involvement in the effort (Own It), determined to figure out the best way to get it done (Solve It), but then never leave the sidelines to participate in the game (Do It). Hello, Below the Line; goodbye, Key Result.

One of the largest eyewear retailers in the world and a longtime client offers a case in point. A few years ago, the company had made remarkable progress toward clarifying, at every level of its organization, the Key Results it needed to deliver in the coming year. Strategically, it wanted to grow revenue from in-store eye exams. In-store appointments were spotty at best. An optometrist might see three patients in a row, and then sit idly for a couple of hours before the next one arrived. As the company's senior leaders began digging into this problem with focus groups and assessments, they discovered a basic problem. It turned out that front-line sales associates focused almost exclusively on selling eyewear. Few of them considered that patients should get their eyes examined before buying a pair of glasses. The solution seemed obvious. Shift the sales staff's role from "My job is to sell glasses" to "My job is to protect the eye health of every customer." That simple change in role definition had real potential to produce the results they were looking for. Three weeks into the campaign, a senior field leader received a voice mail from one of the store managers in California: "This morning one of our sales associates came to work and noticed that the eye exam calendar was empty. Asking what else he could do to make an impact, he began sorting through our files to find individuals who had missed their eye exams over the past year. He then began calling them. He connected with one woman who said that she could actually come in that afternoon and she'd be bringing her children to have their eyes tested as well. When that family left our store, they had spent nearly $3,000 on exams and products. We closed at a plus seventeen points—exceptional—in our comp sales today." Shared throughout an organization, this can become what we call a "Signature Story." It showed everyone that you can deliver great results when you Do It. In Above the Line Cultures people take such lessons to heart and always look around to see more of reality, consider what needs to be done, and take immediate action to get the results they need to achieve. We'll talk more about this in chapter 9.

Learning from failed attempts to Do It ultimately means helping yourself and others to Do It. It's not enough to spend time seeing, owning, and solving a problem without taking the necessary action to do whatever needs to be done to achieve the desired result. Just as a line separates the behavior needed to deliver on the Key Results from the blame game, an even finer line separates good companies from great ones: the line between Solve It and Do It.

2. Recognize That You're Not Taking Full Accountability Until You Do It

We observed a great example of the need to take full accountability when we worked with Redstone Federal Credit Union (RFCU) of Huntsville, Alabama. The firm's leaders, unwilling to settle for a good or even great performance, set their sights on making RFCU the best company in its industry. With twenty-four branch locations and 830 employees, RFCU had established an outstanding track record over the years, never failing to hit its numbers. On paper, it looked perfectly healthy:

- Net worth? *Well above the required level for a well-capitalized credit union: Check.*
- Membership growth? *Average of nine hundred new members each month for nearly seven years: Check.*
- Employee satisfaction? *Employee turnover half of the industry average: Check.*

Why on earth would the company tinker with its formula for success? Because RFCU's leaders wanted even *better* results. Knowing that even a minor, seemingly insignificant little problem could snowball into a bigger one, they decided to convert even the smallest obstacles into opportunities for growth. An extensive internal survey led to two important discoveries: (1) many of the company's departments functioned in silos, with little or no interaction among key departments, and (2) members of the leadership team were not perfectly aligned behind the company's mission.

The RFCU senior leadership team, led by CEO Joe Newberry, decided to build a corporate Culture of Accountability, using the approach you will find in chapter 9 of this book (and in our book *Change the Culture, Change the Game*). Building such a culture meant getting every employee, from the CEO to the staff at large, to take accountability to think and act in the manner necessary to deliver results. At this point, RFCU, after having worked with Partners In Leadership on creating organizational accountability, invited PIL to help with its cultural transition, which resulted in an historic tipping point for the organization. A series of workshops led by key RFCU executives implemented the Steps to Accountability to create a company-wide commitment to achieving best-in-class status in the industry. To communicate that commitment in a clear and tangible way, they collected every single one of the organization's grievances and complaints and wrote them down on a large hatchet-shaped paper. Then they buried that hatchet. Literally.

Within six months, RFCU's already good-to-great culture became even greater. Cross-functional communication to make sure everyone could See It became a daily cultural trait, and every leader and manager aligned behind the mission to become best in class. Feedback gathered from those cross-functional exchanges led to a variety of actions that accelerated improved performance throughout the company. None of that would have counted for much, of course, unless it produced results, and produce results it did. In every area where the company measured success in terms of "threshold, target, or maximum," they quickly began hitting "maximum" on all of them. The most important measure, financial benefits to RFCU's customers, rose dramatically as the Culture of Accountability took hold and flourished at every level in the organization. Here's a quick list of the impressive financial impact from three years of preculture work to three years of postculture work and stepping up to Do It:

- 55 percent growth in annual noninterest income
- 1,052 percent increase in loans
- 1,179 percent increase in average annual total member give-back (excluding dividends)
- 7,251 percent increase in average annual cash-back rebates given to members
- $33,791,007 in member rewards consisting of dividends, rebates/promotions, giveaways, cash back reduced fees, lower loan rates, and so on.

3. Make the Do It Question Part of Every Meeting

Does the following scenario describing Gerald's team seem familiar? On a typical Tuesday morning at 9:30, Gerald's team has assembled for a weekly production meeting. Gerald has spent six years leading these meetings with a furrowed brow and a jarring tone that approaches a scream whenever the team has failed to hit its numbers. This is one of those almost screaming days.

Gerald shouts his displeasure. "All right, you guys, we've got a big problem! I apologize for not sending out the agenda earlier, but I have been buried under an avalanche, trying to catch up on paperwork while putting out fires everywhere I look." He peers around the room. "Somebody's missing. Rick! Where's Rick? Does anyone know where Rick is?"

Everyone smirks because Rick is *always* late.

"We can't wait! Now, about last week's production run. It was a disaster! I mean a *total disaster*. Joe, take us through the numbers."

Joe begins with a slideshow. "I've got eighty-four slides. Slide one shows . . ."

Five minutes later Joe is still droning on, unaware that Gerald's face has turned bright red and everyone else in the room is poking at their phones or lightly snoring.

After twenty minutes, Joe finally wraps up his merciless barrage of charts.

Gerald glowers at him. "Thanks, Joe, for all that detail. So, any questions, you guys?"

Silence.

Gerald looks at his watch. "Ouch, sixty minutes. Okay. Time's up! We'll dive deeper into this next week. Now, let's get back to work. Work harder! Get it done!"

Have you ever attended a meeting like Gerald's, packed with sound and fury but signifying nothing? Don't you love them? Probably not. Over the years we've heard more complaints about unproductive meetings than any other facet of corporate life. Need to boost production? Let's have a meeting. First-quarter sales fell short of quota? Our next meeting will cover that. Want healthier items on the cafeteria menu? Put it on the meeting agenda. Meetings, meetings, meetings and not a minute to spare.

We call it "meeting fatigue." Whether you meet in person, on a conference call, or at the dinner table, it sometimes seems as if work life has become an endless round of meetings where perhaps 10 percent of the agenda helps move you closer to getting the results you need. How do you cope with the problem? "Let's set up a meeting to talk about holding too many meetings."

If you record a typical meeting, you will probably find that it ran over the allotted time, followed an agenda with too many items, did not cover all of those items, and ended with no one knowing what to do and by when to deliver the Key Results.

We haven't counted the number of meetings we've attended in our own company and in organizations around the world over the years, but the total would run into the tens of thousands. We've met with senior executives, middle managers, and front-line workers. Some meetings ran fifteen minutes, some a few hours, and some several days at an executive retreat. Along the way we've come up with a few tips for getting the most out of any meeting. Have we ever planned or conducted a perfect meeting? No. But we have managed to make them shorter, more focused, and more productive. Less "talk about it" and more actual "Do It" is the key. Every meeting has a culture that's created by the person leading that meeting. If you need to improve your meeting culture, we suggest the following:

1. Make sure that the appropriate people are invited to the meeting. Consider the decisions that need to be made and the input that will be needed and invite attendees accordingly.

2. Since leaders, not teams, make decisions, make sure the decision makers are identified and in the meeting.

3. Set a specific time limit. Consider making the time frame shorter than what is normally set given the expectations for the meeting. One executive we know places his watch in the center of the conference table and sets the alarm to ring in one hour. After doing this a few times he shared with us, "People keep an eye on the watch. The first time we met this way, we didn't get through the full agenda. The next time we finished on time. The third time, we wrapped things up with ten minutes to spare. The watch reminds people to focus on Key Results."

4. Make sure the meeting does not end without answering the Do It question: "Who will do what by when?"

5. Determine, while still in the meeting, how decisions will be communicated outside the meeting.

6. Ask participants in the meeting to correlate their to-do lists with the Key Results.

7. Create the expectation for follow-through by scheduling a Return and Report time.

8. Use the framework and common language of accountability. "Bob, I think we may be going Below the Line. Team, let's work Above the Line and make sure we're focused on what else we can do to achieve the Key Results."

These suggestions will be helpful as you work on improving your meeting cultures. As you implement them, don't be surprised if people begin looking forward to your meetings instead of dreading them.

4. Never Stop Until You Achieve the Key Results

Late at night back in 1978 an engineer was working in his garage on a way to enhance computer databases that could rival offerings from IBM and other large suppliers. Two years later, the engineer's hard work met with big success when his company, Teradata, sold its first system to a large East Coast company. That accomplishment prompted a huge celebration among Teradata's employees, who had worked together as a close-knit family for two long years. Finally, all their blood, sweat, and tears was about to pay off.

It was Saturday morning in the parking lot of the Teradata facility, the renovated warehouse that had replaced the garage. A group of fifty-two excited employees and their families were holding balloons and waving banners with the slogan "Ship the Big One." Everyone was wearing a special T-shirt emblazoned with the words *The Big One* on the front and back.

The American Van Lines driver who had been contracted to deliver the shipment couldn't help but catch the excitement from the festivities as he climbed into the cab of his 18-wheeler. As the driver started his engine and pulled out of the parking lot with The Big One aboard, the Teradata families cheered wildly. Moved by the moment, the driver waved back, shouting that he would not let them down. Indeed, the driver felt as if he'd joined the Teradata family, if only for this one haul. His strong sense of ownership in Teradata's first major achievement was palpable and heartfelt.

Almost eight hours into his trip, the driver pulled into his first weigh station only to discover that his load weighed five hundred pounds more than the legal limit. He knew the overweight problem would require a lot of paperwork and approvals that could cause a full day's delay and prevent Teradata from meeting its promised delivery date.

You can probably imagine how easy it might have been for the driver to fall Below the Line, blaming the company for the overweight problem. After all, it wasn't his fault. You can also imagine how easy it might have been for the driver to check into a motel to await further instructions.

However, the driver stayed Above the Line by choosing to do something to solve the problem. After all, the Teradata family was depending on him. What could he possibly do before the sun sets in the west? After some quick thinking, he turned the truck around and drove to the nearest truck stop, where he unpacked the truck's winter chains, removed a number of extra water containers and spare chairs, and then hid everything in a nearby ditch under some brush.

Later he recalled thinking of the risk he was taking. He knew he would probably be fired if he lost that equipment. But what's a little risk if he actually saved the day for his newly adopted family? When he returned to the weigh station, the truck weighed fifty pounds below the limit.

The American Van Lines driver made it to the East Coast and delivered The Big One on time.

After hearing about the driver's experience, Teradata congratulated and celebrated him for taking accountability to get the right result. From that point forward, they incorporated his story into the company's employee orientation program as a perfect example of living Above the Line and ultimately, despite the obstacles, taking the final step to Do It.

Getting Accountability Right: Stepping Up to Do It!

1. Many organizations we work with have standardized the Do It question into their meeting agenda to ensure the question is staring everyone in the face for the entire meeting. You can't end the meeting without answering *who will do what and by when.*

2. The manufacturing arm of a medical device company we work with has created a "Stop Doing It List" to help them deliver their results. After generating flip charts full of ideas, they chose six items to put to bed, immediately redirecting time and resources to what mattered most. One of the enemies of Do It is having too much to do.

3. We can share a multitude of examples of leaders who ensure regular Return and Report conversations happen to further cement "who will do what by when" or to adjust existing assignments and timelines.

4. Find ways to encourage and reward risk taking. One client told us she specifically brings up examples of risk taking in meetings and public forums. She was bringing attention to the behavior of pushing the envelope to encourage more of it. Indirectly, she also rewarded risk by consciously doing everything she could to implement her people's good ideas.

Chapter Seven

ABOVE THE LINE LEADERSHIP

Holding Yourself and Others Accountable for Results

We believe that each of us, irrespective of our position or title, leads others. In fact, leadership is often defined and determined by the amount of influence we have on others. Emmett C. Murphy, author of *Leadership IQ*, describes it this way, "Every worker leads; every leader works." In a sense, accountability is a 360-degree value proposition in which leaders throughout an organization hold both themselves and others accountable for results. That's not easy to implement if a leader clings to the punitive applications of accountability in which people are punished for mistakes or penalized for taking risks and failing to succeed. Even leaders who see *The Oz Principle* application of accountability as a powerful force for getting results can mistakenly find themselves trying to force their newfound wisdom on others, alienating rather than motivating them to take greater accountability for results. If leadership is an art, then Above the Line leadership is the ultimate art form.

Over the last three decades we have worked with thousands of leaders at every level in organizations throughout the world. We've seen the good, the bad, and the ugly, but the Above the Line leaders always find a way to successfully coach others Above the Line.

How Do Above the Line Leaders Coach Others Above the Line?

First and foremost, who is the most important person to get Above the Line? Hopefully, you just answered saying, "I am!" Above the Line leaders work, act, and live Above the Line. Because they do, they quickly recognize when others have become stuck Below the Line. Above the Line leaders know that persistent excuses, explanations, justifications, confusion, denial, and everything else that corresponds with Below the Line attitudes and mind-sets will severely impair an organization's ability to achieve its Key Results. Helping people move Above the Line requires patience and perseverance. Not always easy. When something goes wrong we want to fix it. We want to solve the problem. And we want to solve it now. Oftentimes, it just feels easier to tell people what to do to get back on track. The damaging downside of telling people what to do is that it slows rather than accelerates the growth of individuals, teams, and entire organizations. Facing that reality requires courage. Results depend not only on your working Above the Line but also on getting others to do the same.

Results depend on everyone operating Above the Line.

Above the Line leaders don't sit back and say, "Look, you've messed this up. You need to fix it. Right now. Or else." That approach simply motivates people to hide, point the finger of blame, or make every excuse in the book for what went wrong.

So how do you coach people to take accountability in a way that motivates them to do their best to overcome the obstacles that block the path to achieving Key Results? This may not be easy, but you will find it a lot less painful and much more effective if you apply the LIFT Accountability Coaching model.

The LIFT Accountability Coaching Model

- Listen for obstacles (See It).
- Identify the obstacles you can influence (Own It).
- Facilitate the Solve It question (Solve It).
- Test for movement (Do It).

The leader of a product quality team at a medical supplies company gathered his people on the plant floor a week after beginning *The Oz Principle* Accountability Process. With machines clattering in the background he posed a question that had been haunting him for days. "Can anyone tell me why we have been seeing an uptick in the number of IV bags that fail our quality-assurance tests?" The team immediately started rattling off reasons for the rise in defects, ranging from "The extreme humidity this summer has affected the robotics" to "It's the supplier's fault! We're not getting the best polyvinyl chloride." He looked around the shop floor. "So, all these reasons lead us to one conclusion. We're likely to keep cranking out too many defective IV bags for the foreseeable future. Is that right?" Heads nodded in agreement.

A Below the Line leader might have adjourned the meeting right there and reported up the chain of command that "We don't have the budget to fix everything that has been affecting product quality." But the product quality team leader had made a conscious decision to model Above the Line leadership. Rather than accepting all the excuses for why the problem was happening, he swept aside the curtain. "Look, no wizard is going to pull some magic levers to get us out of this jam. We're smart guys. We *see* the problem. We need to *own* it. Corporate is not going to give us more resources. It's our job to *Solve It* within our current budget. And we need to *Do It* before the end of this quarter. What else can we do to get quality back on track? I've got a couple ideas myself, but I want to hear from you first."

Note that he did not blast his team for engaging in Below the Line excuse making and finger-pointing. Rather, he affirmed his confidence in their problem-solving ability. Nor did he order his people to "fix the problem or else!" He presented the challenge and invited his team to See It, Own It, Solve It, and Do It.

"Before we open up the discussion, I'd like to show you something." He tacked the Steps to Accountability poster on the bulletin board. "Look at this line in the middle. I'm afraid we've been stuck Below the Line on this issue. Now we need to climb Above the Line." He took only three minutes to review and explain the model. Some people had been trained on it, others hadn't, but they all loved it.

"Okay, let's get to it. First, I want to understand everything that is getting in our way of delivering on our production targets. You have said that the humidity this summer has affected the robotics. You've also said we're having problems with our supplier giving us polyvinyl chloride that isn't up to our standards, right? Tell me what else is getting in our way." Then he listened as they raised other obstacles they were facing. He didn't make them feel that he was in a hurry to get to solutions. He genuinely wanted to know what else was getting in their way. He wanted his team to get Above the Line by reengaging them in finding new solutions. Above the Line leaders take step one and listen with empathy.

Listen for obstacles (See It). Above the Line leaders commit to hearing what others are thinking. They want to know what's getting in the way of achieving the needed results and they want it all out on the table. It takes time to dig deep and really hear what's on the minds of an entire team. Above the Line leaders convince others that they really want to hear the truth. They listen intently, withhold judgment, and ask for clarification as needed. They keep Superman's cape in mothballs, never swooping in to save the day with their own solutions. They do not solve problems for their people; they coach their people Above the Line, enabling them to reengage their hearts and minds so *they* feel responsible for discovering the needed solutions.

> *People take great pride in solving problems on their own.*

Our experience has taught us that people actually want to get Above the Line and figure out how to solve problems themselves. The need that many have is simply to feel "heard" during the process of problem solving. Beware, however, of the gravitational pull of Below the Line thinking. An empathetic listener can get so wrapped up in tales of victimhood and woe that they find themselves slipping Below the Line and commiserating there with everyone else. For example, a leader might say to a team member who excuses her consistent tardiness because she is grappling with child custody issues at home, "I get it. That's a terrible thing that's been happening to you. Don't worry about it. It's not your fault." When such feelings arise, it's a good idea to say to yourself, "This person is hurting. I understand how she feels. I need to let her get it all out, then nudge her to take accountability for getting to work on time. I need to help her See It."

After the product quality leader listened to his team, and confirmed they had put all of the obstacles they were facing on the table, he continued by asking, "Which of all of these obstacles that we just talked about can we do something about?"

Identify the obstacles you can influence (Own It). Above the Line leaders help people move from See It to Own It. They do this by encouraging others to identify and prioritize the obstacles they can actually control. Sometimes it helps to list what's in and outside of the team's control. The product quality team compiled the following list:

Can't Control or Influence	Can Control or Influence
Humid Weather	High Humidity in the Plant
Economic Downturns	Costs
Retirement, Illness, and Death	Talent Recruitment
Disruption in the Marketplace	Product Innovation

You can't control what happens in the first column, but you can take charge of what happens in the second column. When the humid weather issue was identified as an obstacle that they could influence or control, one team member proudly offered a possible solution, "I've been looking into the new organic dehumidifiers that use a technologically advanced silica gel."

"Bravo. Inside every problem lurks an opportunity," said the product quality leader.

Another team member said, "A well-known mantra at Amazon is to say nothing about the 'competition' and talk only about what can be done to improve the customer experience. We should stop talking about humidity and only talk about finding the best dehumidifiers."

The team laughed out loud, but they all got it. After that, they identified two other obstacles that they needed to tackle. One was finding a new valve supplier to enhance IV solution flow in and out of the IV bags. Another was recruiting new talent into the engineering staff in anticipation of imminent retirements and the new innovations.

Every Above the Line leader knows that nothing will empower people more than a sense of control and influence over their circumstances free from the debilitating effects of victimhood. That's why Above the Line leaders help people separate the uncontrollable from the controllable, inviting their teams to stop focusing on the former and own the latter.

Facilitate the Solve It question (Solve It). With ownership established, you can move to the Solve It step. As you'll recall from chapter 5, this simple yet powerful question drives the most effective, most innovative, and most productive solutions to the problems you face. It automatically throttles the time-wasting, energy-sapping, unproductive, and costly victim thinking that keeps people stuck Below the Line. When the weather, the economy, or a competitor's disruptive innovation makes the going tough, people who take accountability to Solve It get tougher, continually asking, "What else can I do?"

We've come across rather chronic cases of Below the Line thinking that resist taking this step. Think about this for a minute. When someone is really stuck Below the Line, what are they looking to do? They are looking to explain and justify why they are there. It's actually the path of least resistance to stay there. You clearly need a catalyst to produce movement Above the Line. In such cases, we suggest having those who are stuck imagine that their lives completely depend on finding a solution. It sounds something like this: "Let's just imagine for a moment that your life depended on finding a solution. *What else could you do to solve this problem?*" While their lives more than likely do not depend on finding a solution, this question often stimulates needed creativity, engagement, and rethinking. Sometimes jarring someone out of the habitual Below the Line thinking requires a little jolt to their psyche. "What if your life depended on it?" can provide that jolt. Regardless of the situation you face, circumstances will not likely improve until you have coached everyone to pack away their excuses for poor results and put on their best thinking caps, asking over and over and over again, "What else can I do to get the result we need?"

After a vigorous discussion of what else they could do to overcome the three major obstacles they had identified, the product quality leader interrupted the team and asked, "So what are we going to do?"

The team responded by reviewing the three best ideas they came up with to address the major obstacles and ensure increased error-free production before the end of the quarter. They agreed to put an implementation plan together by the end of the week and present it to him for feedback and approval.

Test for movement (Do It). When someone is Below the Line and looking for someone else to take accountability for finding a solution, Above the Line leadership resists the temptation to tell them what to do and instead focuses on reengaging the mind of the person in looking for the solutions themselves. The LIFT Accountability Coaching Model is not a problem-solving tool. It's really a reengagement tool. Success is found with LIFT when people have moved Above the Line and are reengaged in solving the problem.

When testing for movement, if the team or individuals respond by saying something like, "I (we) just don't know what to do," Above the Line leaders have the patience to begin again. They Listen. Identify. Solve. Test. More often than not, people will move and reengage.

Back at the medical supplies company, our product quality leader ends the highly productive team meeting by saying, "I like the three solutions we've developed. So, let's make sure we are clear on 'Who is going to do what, by when?' Right now, it looks like Jeff is going to obtain a report on the innovative dehumidifiers by the end of the week. Jill will bring back quotes for American-made valves by next Friday. And, I will make sure that HR begins identifying three solid candidates to replace Therese, the engineer retiring next month. Once we've taken these three steps, we'll reconvene to develop more detailed plans for implementation and progress tracking."

As we saw in chapter 6, movement toward the right result depends on everyone knowing the answer to the fundamental question, *"Who will do what by when?"* No matter how smoothly things are going today, new obstacles will arise tomorrow, problems will need to be faced, and speed will be of the essence. But Above the Line leaders will always take the time to get people to engage their own minds and begin looking for solutions. Such leaders recognize that LIFTing their people Above the Line will not only lead to better solutions but also create a team culture of engagement that brims with problem solvers.

Above the Line Leadership Principles

In our experience, Above the Line leaders get the most out of the LIFT model when they do two things really well:

1. Keep People Focused on What Matters Most.
2. Model Above the Line Behaviors.

1. Keep People Focused on What Matters Most

The conductor of a symphony orchestra can't prevent every single distraction that comes along during a performance, but she can choose to ignore the distractions that arise and keep the members of the orchestra focused on the music. Above the Line leaders do the same thing; they choose to ignore the distractions that pointlessly divert attention and instead take accountability to keep their teams focused on what matters most: achieving the Key Results. Whenever someone raises a hand to complain about a problem, an Above the Line leader always asks, "Is this a problem that will get in the way of achieving our Key Results?" If it's a problem they can set aside for now, they set it aside. If, however, the problem will impede achieving the Key Results, then the Above the Line leader gets the team engaged in determining what else can be done to Solve It.

Some years ago, we observed the career of an exceptional leader and cofounder of a highly profitable company. In his midfifties, this talented leader, whom we'll refer to as Mark to protect his privacy, and his partner decided to sell their company to a private equity firm that had submitted the best offer. Mark and his partner felt comfortable selling to the private equity firm because they believed the new owner would give them the best options for rewarding those who would remain behind to manage and grow the business.

When the company was purchased, Mark felt like a parent dropping his daughter off at college and hoping she would be all right. It wasn't easy letting go of the company he'd cofounded. He missed the people he associated with and worked hard to maintain relationships with as many as he could. Over the next couple of years, he observed the business from afar. In terms of sales and profitability, things unfolded pretty much as he expected. But in terms of the people he cared so much about, many of them were not happy. He encouraged them to hang in there while the new owners learned for themselves how to run the business. Then, during the third year after the sale, the company he'd cofounded started to stall. For the first time since 2001 the company wasn't growing. It had missed its numbers two quarters in a row, and the next two quarters looked equally bleak. With the dip in performance and pressure to turn things around, panic set in and morale got worse. The CEO who had replaced Mark and his partner came under increasing pressure from the owner and decided to quit because of mounting stress and failing health.

The company's CFO took over as CEO, and after a few months of continuing poor performance and careful assessment, the new CEO decided to call Mark. He asked Mark to speak to the company as they began the new year. The CEO wasn't exactly sure what he was looking for Mark to do or say, but he knew that if anyone could breathe hope and optimism back into the company, Mark could. Mark was never one to sit idly by while his former colleagues and friends struggled. He wanted to help restore the legacy of the company he worked for so many years to build, so he eagerly accepted the CEO's invitation to speak at the company's upcoming annual kickoff meeting.

Prior to the meeting Mark began reaching out to senior leaders in the company in an effort to understand what they were thinking about the company's current malaise. He got an earful. "Too many new initiatives have taken us away from our brand identity as the leader in our industry. Too many recent hires lacked the needed skills to grow the business. Management had messed up and redesigned the compensation system not once, not twice, but three different times. People are confused and wondering if they will ever see a bonus again. The new owners have no idea how to run our business and their short-term focus has everybody looking over their shoulder." The litany of woes went on and on.

Mark took it all to heart and put a lot of careful thought into the speech he was about to deliver. When he entered the large conference room, he was genuinely determined to help his former colleagues and friends reengage by remembering what they had previously achieved and choosing to be optimistic about their future. After listening to the CEO kick off the meeting by describing the results the company needed to deliver in the coming year, it was time for Mark to do what he had come to do. Mark walked out among the members of the team, looking around at a sea of both familiar and new faces. The veterans knew him as a strong leader; the new people only knew him as one of the company's cofounders.

Mark began with a powerful assertion about their business proposition and its relevance in the current business environment. He did not spend any time telling the people how good it felt to be back. He didn't need to. Everyone could tell. He spoke as if he still owned the business. He engaged with the audience, told success stories, and attempted to ignite the company's imagination once again. He confronted the Below the Line excuses he'd heard that attempted to explain and justify why the company wasn't growing for the first time in sixteen years. He called on the team to get Above the Line and build upon the legacy they had helped create. Then, hesitating for just a moment, he said, "The company I know doesn't go Below the Line! The company I know works Above the Line! The company

I know constantly focuses on what else we can do to achieve our Key Results!"

Everywhere he looked, Mark saw expectant faces, a lot of heads shaking, and more than a few worried expressions. Then he raised his voice and with a clenched fist shouted, "I hope you are not here just biding your time. If you don't want to help us move forward, recapture our momentum, and deliver our Key Results, then get out of here! At this company we achieve our KEY RESULTS!"

You could have heard a feather drop on the floor. The CEO later acknowledged that Mark had forced him to look deeply into a giant mirror. "I felt really uncomfortable because what I saw staring back at me was the ugly reflection of a victim and excuse maker. Frankly, that hurt." Mark had not only performed a masterful piece of cheerleading but also thrown a bucket of ice water on the company's leaders. The experience lit a new fire in their bellies. They were now ready to do whatever it took to put a different reflection in that mirror: the face of a team taking accountability to achieve its Key Results.

Almost instantly, people stopped wasting time, making excuses, pointing their fingers at others for causing their problems, and bemoaning circumstances beyond their control. If you could have eavesdropped on the conversations that leaders held with their people after that breakthrough meeting, you would have heard the common language of positive and propelling accountability in every sentence. You would have heard people choosing to be optimistic. And you would have heard those magic words calling for new action: "At this company we achieve our Key Results."

We can't move on from this story without letting you know that throughout the year the company moved forward with optimism and delivered the highest revenue and EBITDA (earnings before interest, taxes, depreciation, and amortization) numbers in the history of the company. It was a historic and remarkable turnaround.

2. Model Above the Line Behaviors

There's great wisdom in the axiom "Do as I do, not just as I say." Above the Line leaders model Above the Line behaviors. If you don't model Above the Line behaviors you expect from your people, they will only go through the motions while you're in the room, then slip back Below the Line when you leave. Hammer them with the old approach to accountability, using coercion and threats of punishment to keep people on the track toward Key Results, and they will beat each other up with excuses and finger-pointing when anything goes wrong. Coercion and finger-pointing may make leaders and followers feel better about their situations in the short term, but it will do nothing to help them get Above the Line. Of course, it's okay to let people spend a little time venting their emotions. However, as quickly as possible, begin modeling *The Oz Principle* approach to harnessing accountability as a powerful, propelling force in the quest to achieve Key Results. In the long run, that's how Above the Line leaders facilitate movement in the needed direction and make people feel better and more productive at the same time. They engender trust by working effectively Above the Line to do their jobs, fulfill their leadership roles, and achieve the Key Results.

They consistently ask these important questions both of themselves and of their respective teams:

- Are we practicing true accountability? Am I?
- Are we moving toward the Key Results we must achieve? Am I?
- Are we acknowledging the full reality of this situation? Am I?
- Do we accept our impact on this reality? Do I?
- What else can we do to get the results we need? What else can I do?
- Who will do what by when? What will I do by when?

Jack Welch, the highly respected former CEO of General Electric who influenced a generation of business leaders, offers a strong role model for Above the Line leaders who aspire to greatness. As Noel Tichy and Stratford Sherman recount in their seminal book *Control Your Destiny or Someone Else Will,* Jack Welch transformed General Electric into a world-class results generator by modeling his own form of true accountability: "The remarkable story of GE's transformation teaches lessons essential for the well-being of managers and laypersons alike. 'Control your destiny' is more than a useful business idea. For every individual, corporation, and nation, it is the essence of responsibility and the most basic requirement for success. As the world endlessly changes, so must we. The greatest power we have is the ability to envision our own fate—and to change ourselves." That's just another way of describing Above the Line leadership. Throughout his years as GE's leader, Welch stressed the essential values of "self-confidence, candor, and an unflinching willingness to face reality, even when it's painful."

Like all leaders, he encountered his share of challenges and made many missteps along the way: "I've made my share of mistakes—plenty of them—but my biggest mistake by far was not moving faster. Pulling off an old Band-Aid one hair at a time hurts a lot more than a sudden yank. Of course, you want to avoid breaking things or stretching the organization too far—but generally, human nature holds you back. You want to be liked, to be thought of as reasonable. So, you don't move as fast as you should. Besides hurting more, it costs you competitiveness." Then he adds, "When you're running an institution like this, you're always scared at first. You're afraid you'll break it. People don't think about leaders this way, but it's true. Everyone who's running something goes home at night and wrestles with the same fear: Am I going to be the one who blows this place up? In retrospect, I was too cautious and too timid."

Courage. That's the first behavior we stressed in this book when we urged you to muster the courage to acknowledge the reality of your situation. That's what Above the Line leaders do. They are courageous, take heart, and employ their brains, all to consistently exhibit a relentless will to See It, Own It, Solve It, and Do It.

Getting Accountability Right: Lead Out and Lift Others

1. We worked with the chief legal officer of a Catholic-owned health-care system in Illinois who actually paid a framing company to frame a flip chart full of candid feedback that he had received from the other functional teams that interacted with his team. He sent a message that could not be misunderstood: "We're

not hiding from any feedback that we receive, and we plan to act on it because we want to Do It right."

2. Denis Meade, director of training and development for Allo-Source, a leading nonprofit tissue bank, told us, "What gets measured gets attention. So, to have your teams and company do better, find the right metrics and start measuring and reporting."

3. A large government program was stalling out. The program director replaced the agenda of his next meeting with the four steps Above the Line. She asked four questions, one at a time, and captured the answers. Question 1, what do we need to see that we're not seeing today? Question 2, how and where do we need to get more involved? Question 3, what else can we do? Question 4, who needs to do what and by when? Sound familiar? She took her lead from the previous chapters in this book. After 90 minutes, she walked away with what she referred to as the most direct and clear plan they had developed in months. With her deliberate and Above the Line leadership, they put the program back on target by the end of the year.

4. A director of human resources for a digital scanning equipment manufacturer implemented a personal practice he's found very effective when helping colleagues stay Above the Line. Whenever he's in a conversation with a manager or leader, he thinks to himself: *Wait, wait, wait . . . listen, listen, listen.*

Chapter Eight

ABOVE THE LINE TEAMS

Taking Accountability for Team Results

Imagine you're playing third base on the Boston Red Sox, battling
the New York Yankees in the American League Championship Series for the right to move on to the World Series. Your team hasn't
won a game. Your archrival has won three. At the time, no team in
the history of Major League Baseball has ever come back from such
a deficit. What would you do? Give up and go home so you could
mope around feeling sorry for yourself and licking your wounds?
Not if you are an Above the Line team. Such a team would find the
heart and the courage and the brains to do what no one else has ever
done. And that's exactly what the Red Sox did in 2009 when they
executed a stirring comeback, fighting their way back into conten-
tion and winning the seventh and deciding game by a score of 10–3.
It's amazing what a team can do when the players refuse to give up
and instead take accountability for what happens next. A similar
thing happened to the Cleveland Cavaliers in 2016 when they came

back from a 3–1 deficit to win the NBA Championship. Above the Line teams do not give up!

How Do You Keep Your Team Above the Line?

You may not play for a professional sports franchise, but you likely play on a lot of teams every day. Take a data analyst in a midsize company whose role touches multiple divisions, including the marketing team, operations team, and the IT team. After work, she plays on the family team, her athletic club's tennis team, and her church's fund-raising team. In many instances, life, as it turns out, is all about teams. And it's a two-way street. Your team supports you; you support your team. As Winston Churchill famously said, "We shape our buildings; thereafter they shape us." Any team that wants to win, no matter its current level of performance, must figure out how to shape their team so that it instinctively rises Above the Line and then stays there while focusing all of its energy on delivering results.

Even in this era of dynamic, disruptive change, we still hear people say, "You can't swim upstream," "You can't beat the system," "Don't rock the boat," or "You can't fight City Hall." Those are nothing but weak justifications for settling for the status quo. What if the 2009 Red Sox had packed their bags, mentally, after the third loss? They would have failed. What about the data analyst we mentioned? Because she worked so effectively helping the teams she touched stay Above the Line, she rose in the ranks to manager, director, and then vice president. What if she had just gone through the motions at work watching others move up the ladder? She would not have experienced the growth and fulfillment in work that she has. Above the Line team players take accountability for their futures and for the futures of their teams. Whatever game you're playing, on the field, at work, or in so many other endeavors, Above the Line teams take accountability to rise above their circumstances and deliver results.

Above the Line teams incorporate the common language of accountability into their daily interactions. Early in her career, the data analyst had received feedback from an operations team leader that set her on the right path. The operations leader had said, "Your explanation for the gap in our data retrieval system could keep us Below the Line. I need you to make sure we really *see* and *own* the reality of what's happening there and stay focused on getting the result we need." When you're playing on a team and you're looking to propel it forward, keep the Steps to Accountability model foremost in your mind. Put it on the back of a calling card you can keep in your wallet or obtain a poster you can tack to the wall of a conference room, where it can remind you and everyone else to consistently practice Above the Line thinking and Above the Line behaviors.

Another strong team leader we recently observed in action devoted time at the beginning of each and every team meeting to hear success stories from his direct reports. The positive experiences his people shared reinforced the benefits of the Above the Line behaviors he wanted his team to demonstrate. These success stories stressed the importance of the team's movement toward delivering their Key Results. Such positive forms of coaching keep everyone's eyes on the prize. The consistency and frequency of the stories kept everyone looking for the Above the Line behavior they needed to continually recognize in others.

Most people cringe at the idea of attending a half-day meeting, fearing it will more than likely distract them from getting their work done. Why is that? It's because so many meetings expand to fill the allotted time, whether needed or not, and tend to stray into unproductive conversations that do little or nothing to improve the Key Results. As we mentioned earlier, the divisional leadership team of a consulting firm that specializes in project management found a better way to conduct its regular Friday-morning team meetings. The division's president restricted the agenda to items tied directly to Key Results.

The attendees varied from week to week. Each week his leadership team would invite selected people from throughout the division to report on activities related to the division's Key Results. Those invited attendees, knowing that they needed to cover a given topic clearly and succinctly in a specifically allotted time, carefully prepared their presentations. They also knew that the leadership team would analyze their work using the common language of accountability. Did a leader's reaction to an unexpected cost problem represent Below the Line or Above the Line thinking? Did a solution follow the Steps to Accountability (See It, Own It, Solve It, Do It)? The presenters received kudos for a job well done and constructive feedback on what they might have done better.

Everyone benefited from these Above the Line team meetings. The invited attendees received appropriate coaching from the leaders, and the leaders gained insight into areas where they needed to take greater accountability themselves. The leaders also enjoyed an opportunity to give and receive feedback from their peers. We learned that one invited leader brought several members of her project team along to help with the presentation because her previous presentation had sparked a wave of skeptical feedback. Knowing that some division leaders thought her project had gone off track, she organized this new presentation around the specific ways she and her team were taking accountability to improve the project's contribution to Key Results. After she summarized the project's status with well-prepared charts, graphs, and statistical analyses, she invited questions from the division leaders. One of them quickly exclaimed: "I think this project is going south. If you don't fix it, and I mean *this* week, there will have to be changes."

Another leader responded, "I find that assessment a little unfair and possibly Below the Line." The other division leaders immediately nodded their agreement, and the presenter heaved a big sigh of relief. The disapproving leader was frustrated but acknowledged that the others were right. His acknowledgment led to a tightly focused discussion that exhibited the joint accountability necessary to get the project back on track. They used the Steps to Accountability to further assess the status of the project and to coach the project leader and her team toward solving the problems that had been plaguing them. At the end of the session, the formerly disapproving leader extended his hand to the project leader and offered his help. "Look, I got into the same pickle a few years ago. I'll drop by after the meeting and tell you what we did to solve it." Above the Line teams work to keep the team members Above the Line and give them feedback when they slip!

At the conclusion of each meeting the leadership team discussed what happened during the meeting and decided if more reinforcement of the Above the Line thinking was needed to deliver the Key Results. For their part, the project leader and her invited attendees returned to their coworkers with much-needed encouragement for the progress they had made toward the Key Results and the constructive feedback they received that would help them do even better in the future.

When "What else can I do?" replaces "What did I do wrong?" Key Results become easier to achieve. Since victim thinking and the blame game always get in the way, Above the Line teams move as quickly as possible to both recognize and eliminate Below the Line behavior from the equation. That shift gets them moving toward a Culture of Accountability that will guide the team's approach in overcoming whatever obstacles they face in achieving their Key Results.

Get accountability right and you'll get team members doing their work with the sort of "we can do anything" attitude that brought an American League pennant to Fenway Park in 2009. When you infuse your meetings and personal interactions with a positive and propelling brand of accountability, those once-dreaded time-wasting, full of excuse-making, and off-topic conversations fall by the wayside. Constructive feedback replaces corrosive accusations, humility replaces arrogance, and optimism replaces pessimism. When people move from Below the Line to Above the Line, they show up to work at the same location, but they do so with greater energy and enthusiasm. It takes a certain amount of awareness and effort to pull that off, but Above the Line thinking will move your team more steadily toward the results they need to achieve than almost anything else.

Above the Line Team-building Principles

Whether you lead or play on a team, you can rely on three specific principles to help you remain Above the Line and boost performance:

1. Call out Below the Line Thinking and Behavior.
2. Coach Each Other Through Appreciative and Constructive Feedback.
3. Ask Basic Above the Line Questions.

1. Call Out Below the Line Thinking and Behavior

If you've read everything to this point, we assume your team has started embracing the Steps to Accountability and using the powerful, common language associated with those steps as they work and interact with their teammates. If not, then walk your team through the model. Give them copies of the one-page at-a-glance graphic and tack it up on the wall of your meeting room. If they demonstrate more of an appetite, urge them to read this book and download the *Propeller* App. Those who do that or participate in our formal, in-person Accountability Process will gain valuable depth and layers of application of the Steps to Accountability.

Above the Line teams make sure their teams abandon the view of accountability as a way to coerce, threaten, or punish people. This view only stimulates fear. And fear is accountability's number one enemy. We find that almost everyone unfamiliar with our definition describes accountability in negative terms: "Something that happens to you when things go wrong," "Paying the piper," "Explanations for what went wrong," "How management penalizes you when you make a mistake." We'll say it again—stamp out that thinking with *The Oz Principle*'s powerful, propelling definition of accountability:

> A personal choice to rise above one's circumstances and demonstrate the ownership necessary for achieving desired results; to See It, Own It, Solve It, and Do It.

True accountability should govern both individual and team behavior. You apply it to your own work, to one-on-one interactions with a teammate, and to team meetings. Of course, it's always a good idea to praise and reward people for operating Above the Line, but solving problems and getting Key Results almost always depend on calling out instances of Below the Line thinking and behavior.

Teaching and reteaching the Steps to Accountability keeps people from wasting valuable time making excuses and pointing fingers or waiting for the wizard to offer a magical solution to a troublesome situation. To maintain that awareness, we encourage you to conduct a periodic Team Accountability Assessment:

Team Accountability Assessment

Circle the response that best describes your team.

Do you ever hear people blaming others for what goes wrong?

Never   Seldom   Sometimes   Often   Always

Do you feel that people do not accept responsibility for what they do or how they do it?

Never   Seldom   Sometimes   Often   Always

Do people fail to take the initiative to report on their activities and their progress toward results?

Never   Seldom   Sometimes   Often   Always

Do team members fail to "dive for the ball" when it falls on the ground?

Never   Seldom   Sometimes   Often   Always

Do people "wait and see" if things will get better when serious problems pop up?

Never   Seldom   Sometimes   Often   Always

Do you hear people saying they feel a situation is out of their control and that they can do nothing to resolve it?

Never   Seldom   Sometimes   Often   Always

Do people spend time "covering their tails" when things go wrong?

Never   Seldom   Sometimes   Often   Always

Do people talk about their activity and effort rather than results?

Never   Seldom   Sometimes   Often   Always

Do you hear people say, "It's not my job or my department," and act as if they expect someone else to solve the problem?

Never   Seldom   Sometimes   Often   Always

Do you feel that people display a low level of personal ownership and involvement when problems arise?

Never   Seldom   Sometimes   Often   Always

"Sometimes," "Often," or "Always" answers suggest that your team spends too much time operating Below the Line, and if they want to achieve results, they need to get back Above the Line as soon as possible.

One final thought about calling out people for Below the Line thinking and behavior: Beware of the all-too-human temptation to feel a shiver of *schadenfreude* when you bring a slippage to someone's attention. The German word means "deriving pleasure, joy, or self-satisfaction that comes from learning of or witnessing the troubles, failures, or humiliation of another." People can sense when someone harbors such feelings, and that makes them feel as if they are getting whacked upside the head with a punishing hammer, exactly the opposite of the way they should feel when taking true accountability for results. In other words, never use the language that describes Below the Line thinking as a weapon to embarrass team members into moving Above the Line.

2. Coach Each Other through Appreciative and Constructive Feedback

Experts on the subject of team building have written countless books about assembling, managing, and working in high-performance teams, but we want to stress two characteristics of Above the Line teams that greatly enhance performance: inclusion and conflict. When your team includes individuals with different perspectives, backgrounds, and approaches to problem solving, conflicts will naturally erupt. While head-to-head combat and emotionally charged arguments can distract any team from its focus on achieving results, some of the best ideas emerge when people engage in a spirited debate. The cofounders of Partners In Leadership when either writing their books or working with clients would often disagree. But they managed that disagreement with aplomb. One would have an idea on what they should do. The other would have a different idea about what they should do. Rather than allowing these differences to divide them, they learned to take advantage of them. They actually arrived at a place where they relished challenging situations that caused them to disagree. They realized this allowed the two of them, and those who worked most closely with them, to become a very effective Above the Line team. What did they discover? That by remaining Above the Line in their discussions there was always a third and better way than either of their original suggested solutions. By working together and seeking to learn from each other, they refined their process, discovering that the best solutions are usually born out of vigorous debate.

In chapter 7 we explored how Above the Line leaders help others rise and stay Above the Line. Whether you coach the whole team as a group or each team member individually in one-on-one sessions, you should keep addressing the power of accountability to impact the Key Results. Effective coaching relies on appreciative and constructive feedback and instills a deep appreciation for the power of accountability.

One of our clients, a hospital administrator who oversees the work of a nurse supervisor, knows that she has a penchant for taking long detours Below the Line. After attending *The Oz Principle* Accountability Training, the hospital administrator challenged the nurse supervisor to try demonstrating more of an Above the Line approach to her work and to report back at the end of her next shift. An actual excerpt from the nurse supervisor's email to her boss is presented below. It's a little lengthy, but we included the excerpt because it shows how constructive feedback in a coaching session can lead to a series of experiences that reinforce the propelling power of accountability. Here's what she wrote:

> During the entire shift, I was trying to ask questions to redirect the focus, instead of agreeing with the group and participating in negative conversations.
>
> As an example, a new employee stated at 11:00 p.m. that she'd had the worst night of her life on Saturday. She felt she'd had no preceptor (shift supervisor) all shift. I wanted to go Below the Line and point out all the ways I and the preceptor interacted with her. Instead, I walked away for twenty minutes, got my head together, and then sought her out. I asked her to talk about how she felt that night, why it was her worst night, and why she felt she had no preceptor. We ended up having a twenty-minute discussion and both felt better.
>
> Later, I asked a staff nurse, "How are you doing?" She replied she was sick of things and was ready to walk out very

soon. She said this in front of people. I didn't want to know what happened. After avoiding her for a few hours, I went back and said, "You seem frustrated. Would you like to tell me about it?" We proceeded to have a good conversation. She apparently had family issues, and it truly wasn't related to work or me.

Yes, I find myself Below the Line a lot, now that I realize what I am doing. For example, I used to leave certain tasks for the next shift to do, but now I am taking accountability for those things and getting them done before I leave.

Assignments: I am able to direct others to talk to the "charge nurse" if the assignment is difficult versus hearing them just complain about it.

I was in a conversation with an employee who was attacking me and my actions. My first reaction was defensive. I then brought myself Above the Line by actively listening and finding what the problem was and then acted on that. I acknowledged that a staff member was busy and that it was a busy day. However, I initially didn't offer assistance to the individual. I reflected and then brought myself Above the Line by giving myself permission to offer help. Thanks for your leadership and help.

Accountability became a dominant theme for both the hospital administrator and the nurse supervisor, a steady drumbeat that dominated their work, day in and day out, for the rest of their careers. It sustained them through the worst of times and further propelled them when things were going well. The nurse supervisor later acknowledged to the hospital administrator, "I now realize that living Below the Line is like battling a terrible cancer with no hope of remission."

3. Ask Basic Above the Line Questions

In each of the chapters of this book we have posed a basic question you should ask as you move through the Steps to Accountability. In chapter 7, where we applied accountability to leadership, we invited you to keep these questions in mind as you develop your skills as an Above the Line leader. Above the Line teams should also make these questions an integral part of their daily work.

Basic Above the Line Questions

- Are we demonstrating true accountability?
- Are we moving toward the Key Results we must achieve?
- Have we acknowledged the full reality of this situation?
- On what issues, relative to our Key Results, have we fallen Below the Line?
- Can we see where we need to be more involved in the face of the current reality?
- What else can we do to get the results we need?
- Who will do what by when?

The Brooklyn district sales manager for a global pharmaceutical company could not believe that the team he recently took over ranked dead last out of the company's fifty-seven districts. As he met with his sales reps to discuss the problem, he heard the usual excuses: "I'm doing everything I possibly can" and "We're not getting the support we need from marketing. And we're not alone in feeling that way. The entire field force is beyond frustrated with marketing!" It seemed as if the team actually believed it would fail. The sales manager shared with us, "I just didn't see a way out of this mess." Then one day he picked up a copy of *The Oz Principle*, a book that a former mentor had recommended he read. As he lay in bed that night, he kept flipping pages until he sat up and exclaimed, "I need to examine my *own* heart. I can't hold my people accountable for getting better results unless I hold myself accountable. When it comes to getting results, I need to model precisely what I expect from others."

That insight led him to ask the basic questions in all team meetings and one-on-one meetings. The team gradually began to think and act with accountability. A year later the district had dramatically improved its sales numbers and expected an even better performance the following year. A new set of beliefs took hold. Once the team members set aside their excuse making, their formerly downcast eyes looked up to see a bright future ahead. Each successive year the team's performance kept improving until the district took home the top performance award in its division. Over the next several years, the sales manager's district never finished out of the top ten. During that time, the company promoted him to regional sales manager and eventually to president of the division. As much as that pleased him, he took even greater pride in the fact that many of his district sales representatives also went on to positions of greater responsibility in the industry. He had created a whole new generation of Above the Line team leaders as a result of leading that younger team to work, act, and live Above the Line.

Remember, as we've advised before, bad things can and do happen to good teams. The economy goes south, customers tighten their belts, disruptive competition changes the game, someone's home life hits the rocks, leadership expects you to do the impossible, you name it. But you cannot let those bad things paralyze you or your team. Above the Line teams take charge of what happens next. They take accountability for achieving their Key Results.

Getting Accountability Right: Teams That Never Give Up

1. The senior leaders at a major pizza company decided to institute culture teams. The teams consist of internationally mixed groups, with five or six members from varying company levels on each. These teams meet once a week to talk about anything and everything, building greater understanding, alignment, and connectedness throughout the company.

2. Three nurse colleagues found themselves frustrated and beaten down by the lack of support they felt from leadership at their hospital. They cared about the patients they served but found themselves increasingly sitting off to the side complaining to each other about all the problems in their unit. After allowing such behavior to gain some momentum over time, one of the nurses spoke up and said, "I think we're spending too much time Below the Line and it doesn't make me feel good." The

others agreed, and they decided right then to start making a difference by taking action in ways they could control to improve their unit. Within six months the unit went from the middle of the pack to leading their hospital in patient satisfaction. Nothing had really changed from the larger organization; they had the same resources and same challenges. However, these colleagues decided to change the culture of their team and it spread like wildfire. Pretty soon everyone wanted to work in that unit.

3. The operations VP of a cybersecurity company brought two dysfunctional departments together by taking them bowling. Once the two groups made it onto the bus alive, they started talking. Small talk. Real conversations broke out. Barriers started to drop. Bowling became a monthly ritual.

4. The CEO of a travel company and the most successful high school rugby coach in the United States implemented a "why" and "what" to cross-functional collaboration. "The key to team wins is for everyone in each position to understand what the other positions are doing and why they're doing it."

Chapter Nine

ABOVE THE LINE CULTURES

Creating the Ultimate Organizational Advantage

A major defense contractor headquartered in the southwestern United States retained us to help it solve what the company's CEO called "the worst train wreck in our history." Our initial phone interview tried to pinpoint the problem. We asked him, "What is the number one obstacle blocking your path to better results?" The CEO answered almost before we finished the question.

"MMSI has gone off the rails."

"MMSI?"

"Materials Management System Implementation, or MMSI, pronounced 'Missy' around here."

As we dug into the MMSI situation, we heard the same response from every key leader. "We've spent eighteen months and millions of dollars trying to get this system up and running, and the harder we push her, the worse it gets." Everything depended on MMSI behaving properly, because the company needed the precise inventory data only it could provide, allowing leaders to make crucial manufacturing decisions affecting the future of their company. Remaining profitable and competitive depended on MMSI functioning the way it should.

The company's CFO put it succinctly, "We've been relying on a twenty-year-old inventory system. We need accurate real-time data on everything, and if we don't get the data, we'll end up with manufacturing delays that we just cannot afford." The old system had been limping along, but the company that had built it in the first place had gone through so many mergers and acquisitions that it no longer provided adequate support to keep it running smoothly. What's worse, the supplier recently told the company they were going to completely eliminate its support in the near future. Going forward, the defense contractor and the Old System would be on their own.

Clearly, this defense contractor needed to retire the Old System and get MMSI up and running before the Old System and the potential problems it could create consumed all of the company's profits. Because senior leaders knew that their future depended on MMSI, they assumed everyone else understood the importance of MMSI's implementation. They expected that people throughout their organization would line up and help them get it done. However, as we surveyed the company, the data we obtained revealed that people generally did not agree that the new system was needed. People basically chalked up all of the talk about the new system to the "same old ranting from management. They want a shiny new system when the old one works fine." In a nutshell, the company's people believed the following:

1. The Old System has always gotten the job done! We don't need to fix something that's not broken!
2. We can support the Old System ourselves without the supplier's help.
3. MMSI was too complicated to implement in the time allotted to do it.

In short, these beliefs, inaccurate as they were, were aiding and abetting MMSI in running completely off the rails. As we helped the company's leaders understand that these deep-seated beliefs were preventing the company from successfully implementing MMSI, they began to reach out to comprehend the problem more fully. They uncovered a number of interesting developments that were occurring as MMSI was being implemented. As you read this list, pay attention to the underlying connection between the beliefs people hold and the way they act.

- People were sabotaging the project to make the Old System look better.
- Confusion was being expressed at every turn: "I don't get it. MMSI is way too complicated."
- Key meetings were being skipped by critical people on a regular basis.
- Important messaging as to the "why" behind MMSI was not shared beyond the senior levels of the business.
- Every mistake or setback was shared throughout the organization while positive reports of success were largely ignored.

Negative sentiments concerning MMSI had been building for eighteen months. Frustration had turned into disdain. Pessimism ran rampant. No one could find the courage to see the real problem. No one's heart was in the project. And everyone's brain had frozen at the thought of solving the problems associated with its effective implementation.

But here's the really sad part. A little research revealed that thousands of organizations around the world no more complex than the defense contractor had introduced and integrated MMSI without a hitch. Why couldn't their company, whose people were literally rocket scientists and just as smart and hardworking as the employees of any other major corporation, make it work? The answer, in one word, was CULTURE. Clearly these rocket scientists could figure out how to make MMSI work if their beliefs weren't holding them hostage.

Do You Provide the Right Experiences to Shape the Desired Cultural Beliefs?

If a dog bit you as a child, you may as an adult view dogs as dangerous. To change that belief, you will definitely need some new experiences with friendly, tail-wagging dogs that don't sink their teeth into your ankles. That may seem painfully obvious, but when it comes to corporate culture, leaders too often neglect that basic fact of human behavior—experiences create beliefs and our beliefs influence the actions we take. If the commonly held belief in your current culture is that the new lean initiative merely reflects leadership's passion for every new fad that comes along, that belief springs from a set of past experiences. In the eyes of the people assigned the task of implementing the new initiative, there's little reason to put heart and soul into it because the company has jumped on every management bandwagon that has come down the pike, only to set it aside later for the Next Big Thing. People will smile and nod indulgently and go about their work the same old way. To change that belief, you will need to provide experiences that prove the value of the new initiative and leadership's commitment to follow through. Why are we doing this? What results will we enjoy if we implement it well? What will happen if we don't? Shifting these beliefs will require more than a poster campaign. *Leaders can't tell their people to change their beliefs and expect them to do it. Instead, leaders must create the experiences needed to shape the desired new beliefs.*

We show our clients the methodology for creating Above the Line Cultures imbued with accountability by using this simple but powerful model:

Figure 9.1

——————— THE RESULTS PYRAMID ———————

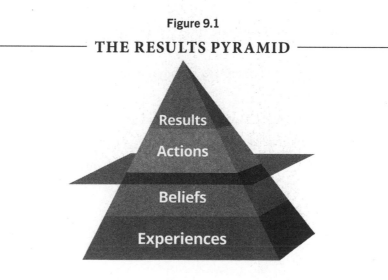

The model is deceptively profound. It suggests that experiences form beliefs, beliefs drive actions, and actions produce results. It also suggests that most leaders only work the top two layers (Actions and Results), while ignoring the bottom two layers (Experiences and Beliefs). Consequently, leaders spend most of their time trying to deliver better results by focusing on the way people are acting. They create new action plans, hang new checklists, rewrite the standard operating procedures, etc., all the while ignoring that the beliefs people hold will ultimately dictate how they behave over the long term.

A lot of leaders toss around the words *culture* and *accountability* without paying much attention to their true meanings. By this point you know we define accountability as a powerful, positive force that propels people toward whatever results they seek. We define culture as the sum total of the experiences, beliefs, and actions that enable an organization to achieve its Key Results.

> *A company's culture is the sum of the experiences, beliefs, and actions that enable it to achieve its Key Results or impede it from doing so.*

The right culture can practically guarantee success; the wrong culture will almost always lead to failure. For years we have worked with leadership teams to grasp and embrace this truth: Either you will manage your culture or it will manage you. We recently worked with a leader in the health-care industry who led the emergency department (ED) of a well-known hospital on the Atlantic Seaboard. Like all hospital emergency operations, her department remained on steady alert and dealt constantly with life-or-death medical crises. The entire ED staff was extremely dedicated, well trained, and competent.

All of them did great work. Nevertheless, the ED administrator wanted to achieve one major Key Result: improve the collection of emergency contact information from a dismal 42 percent to something approaching 100 percent. Why was this important? Suppose Patient A was wheeled into the emergency room with a life-threatening chest wound. The staff would rally to stop the bleeding and save the patient's life. To increase the likelihood of success, they needed to begin by gathering certain vital information, such as blood pressure and heart rate and blood type. Quickly thereafter, they would need some additional but equally vital information about Patient A: her current list of medications, her medical history, her next of kin, any prior surgeries, and so on.

The ED administrator tracked the next of kin information-gathering problem down to its source. The admitting forms, it turned out, were much too complicated and confusing for the harried staff to complete as they worked to save lives. *Aha*, she thought, *I just need to design a much simpler, easy-to-use form!* She carefully crafted the new form and had it translated into all of the major languages spoken by non-English-speaking patients. Once she felt satisfied with it, she arranged for a series of training sessions for her entire staff. Three months had elapsed from the moment she saw the cause of the problem and implemented the solution. She deserves kudos, right? Maybe not. Just look at the results four months after she installed the new admittance forms. The next-of-kin information had limped forward from 42 percent to just 47 percent.

To understand why the results were not forthcoming you need only look to the Results Pyramid. What does a leader ignore when they choose to manage a pyramid that's only two levels deep? In the final analysis, they are ignoring the fact that people think (Beliefs) and that there are reasons for why they think the way they do (Experiences). The ED administrator was devastated with the lack of progress in collecting next-of-kin information. "All that time and effort, and almost no budge in the number. My people are broken!"

Looking at the Results Pyramid, we asked her to consider where she had spent all her time while focusing on improving the collection of next-of-kin information. She quickly observed that she had exclusively concentrated on actions: rewriting forms, conducting training, changing policies, and instructing people to adopt the new process. While focusing on actions, the ED administrator ignored the fact that her people believed that "collecting all that information doesn't help us do better work." She hadn't spent any time at the Beliefs and Experiences levels of the Results Pyramid.

As a result, she could have spent every waking hour for a month training people on her new information-gathering process and seen little overall progress. If she didn't discover and deal with their bedrock belief that gathering next of kin information didn't make a difference, she might as well have been trying to teach them to fly. One of the nurses in the department said something after the training that perfectly summed up the troubling situation: "That was a useful training on gathering emergency contact information. And if I ever need that information, I'll be sure to use the new system." Note the key phrase in the nurse's reaction: "if I ever need that information." Underlying those words is the fundamental belief that, in the heat of battle, collecting that information must take a backseat to everything else. By not starting at the base of the Results Pyramid, the ED administrator had let herself get caught in the "action trap," where leaders mistake a flurry of motions for real movement toward results.

> *Leaders tend to get caught in an action trap*
> *that does little to help people achieve and*
> *sustain results over time.*

Culture Change Principles

When, like the ED administrator, you need to change your people's beliefs in order to achieve a Key Result, you will find these three principles quite helpful:

1. Experiences Change Beliefs.
2. Belief Bias, as Well as the Organizational Narrative, Need to Be Known and Managed.
3. Leaders Must Weave Accountability into the Culture.

1. Experiences Change Beliefs

To change a negative belief that currently blocks your path to Key Results, you need to strike at the cause of that belief. You need to replace the experiences that shaped those beliefs with ones that will inspire people to take the needed actions to get the result. Experiences are created in three ways within an organization: firsthand or face-to-face, from the stories we tell or hear, and from the day-to-day practices, policies, and procedures.

In the case of the ED administrator, she consciously decided to tell two meaningful stories that would cause people to begin to believe that they really did need to collect the expected admissions information. Thinking about the memorable events that had occurred in the emergency department in the past couple of years, she settled on two especially meaningful illustrations of how collecting next-of-kin information could make a lifesaving difference.

Story #1

A college student was wheeled into the ED after a car sideswiped her bike. They did not get her next-of-kin information as they admitted her. While emergency personnel were treating her injuries, she became unconscious and unresponsive. Nothing they tried brought her back. She was gone. They learned shortly after that she had a medical condition that they were completely unaware of. Had they been aware of the condition it would have changed their treatment for her. It may not have ultimately changed the outcome, but it would have greatly increased her chances for survival.

Story #2

When an elderly gentleman was brought into the ED, the staff diligently collected all the necessary information on the admissions form. Shortly after the staff began treating him, his condition mysteriously deteriorated. A quick-thinking nurse found his daughter's phone number on the admissions form and called to ask her if there was anything else the staff needed to know about her father's medical history. "Yes!" exclaimed the daughter. "He had a medical procedure three weeks ago that's not on your list." As they discussed the procedure and the medication he was taking, they quickly realized that what they were treating him with was conflicting with what he was taking. That knowledge sent their approach to treatment down a different path, making sure that what they were administering would not conflict with his current medication. The patient quickly responded to the new course of treatment; they brought him back and saved his life.

Over the next three weeks the ED administrator told and retold these stories to her people. Then she rechecked the numbers to see if they had worked the way she hoped they would. Her heart skipped a beat when she saw the number: a whopping increase from 47 percent to 92 percent. She had escaped the action trap. The experiences she had shared accomplished what all that earnest training had failed to do. It was almost magical. When you create the right experiences, those experiences shape the right beliefs, and people take the right actions to get the results they need. When you work with the entire Results Pyramid and give proper attention to the bottom two layers, Beliefs and Experiences, you create an environment in which people exhibit the desired behaviors—not because policy or procedure requires their participation but rather because needed beliefs drive their actions.

2. Manage Belief Bias and the Organizational Narrative

The Results Pyramid also lends insight into a phenomenon that psychologists call "confirmation bias," the all-too-human inclination to view events as validation of current beliefs. In our practice, we use the term *belief bias*. Here's how it works. If you believe something, you will accept any new data that support your belief without question. If you do not believe something, you will ignore data that suggest you should think differently.

When you create or share experiences designed to shape new beliefs, you must acknowledge that people will view them through the lens of their existing biases. It takes vigilance to spot and cope with those biases. For example, let's say you're driving to work ready for another day of working in accordance with "the way we do things around here." In other words, your belief bias is in alignment with the existing culture. If the company's leaders are striving to create a new Above the Line Culture, they will try to provide Above the Line experiences for you and others that support the new way of thinking and acting. You may find the experiences enlightening, but you and your colleagues can easily fall back into old patterns that keep all of you Below the Line. Let's assume that your boss anticipates that possibility and sits down with you one-on-one, explaining the nature of belief bias and urging you to be open to the changes the company wants people to make in the way they think about and do their work. Your boss says something like, "I'm asking you to look at this culture change initiative through my eyes. I firmly believe that taking personal accountability for the culture shift will be good for you, for our team, and for the whole company because it will dramatically improve our results."

Of course, you cannot just utter the words "You must model Above the Line thinking and acting by personally modeling the new culture" and expect that to be enough. During culture change, staying Above the Line is fraught with pitfalls and obstacles, but nothing can bring the journey to a screeching halt faster than holding on to old belief biases. If you understand how much belief biases shape human behavior and expect to wrestle with making changes to past or current biases in yourself and others, you have already moved halfway toward overcoming them.

We recently helped another large metropolitan hospital implement a process of creating an Above the Line Culture. To measure our success, we looked at fluctuations in Patient Satisfaction Scores, in large part because government reimbursement rates depend on those scores. But Patient Satisfaction Scores also took two Key Results into account: customer experience as well as financial performance. Regrettably, the scores were improving at a snail's pace.

One day early in the engagement, our consulting team interviewed forty-five front-line employees drawn from every major functional area in the hospital. We then incorporated our findings in a major report to the hospital's executive team. As our interviews proceeded, a rather fascinating theme emerged. Almost everyone we interviewed answered our question about the slowly advancing Patient Satisfaction Scores exactly the same way: "We don't have enough head count to get the job done for our patients." In other words, people chalked up the problem to understaffing. "You can't get a hundred gallons of milk out of one cow," said one head nurse with a rueful smile.

When we met with the executive team to share our findings, the staffing explanation bewildered them. "No way," said the CEO. "Our staffing levels are higher than industry norms. And this hospital's nurse-to-patient ratios are third highest in the state."

We explained the paradox. "Your numbers prove that understaffing does not explain the slow progress, but your people still believe it does because that excuse has been fully woven into your organization's culture and narrative." In fact, the narrative had become so deeply entrenched that one nurse told us that she believed that understaffing was a big problem because, in her words, "That's what everyone always says when someone asks about our Patient Satisfaction Scores."

Does that sound familiar? "It's the way we do things around here." The executive team desperately wanted to create a Culture of Accountability, but they weren't going to make that happen unless they dealt with the organizational narrative that sustained the belief that you could chalk up every problem to understaffing. In the common language of accountability, people would not move Above the Line until they abandoned their Below the Line narrative and the beliefs that went along with it. You want to change the culture? Change the narrative.

Belief bias always creates narratives in organizations. At first blush, belief bias can often look daunting, almost insurmountable. That's just not so. You can always overcome belief bias, but it takes deliberate and focused effort applied through an effective, proven process.

Every organization has its narratives, the stories that explain "the way we do things around here" or why such-and-such problems happen. Leaders need to discover and understand those narratives before they attempt to make any meaningful, lasting changes in their organizational culture. We've developed a four-step process that will help you do that.

Rewriting an Organizational Narrative

Step 1: Identify the Narrative

You detect the existing narrative in three ways: listen, listen, and listen. Set aside your own assumptions, put on your humble earphones, and ask people to tell you the stories that support their cultural beliefs. Don't argue or judge or express shock and bewilderment. It may take several conversations before people feel comfortable telling you the unvarnished truth, but your patience will be rewarded with a deeper understanding of what your people really believe and why they believe it. Here's an example of a good response, "Thank you for your honesty about the Patient Satisfaction Scores. I needed to hear that."

Step 2: Share Your Reaction to the Narrative

Once you have learned the narrative, let your people know what you think about it. State your reaction in a positive way, making sure you do not express anger or ridicule even if you think the narrative represents Below the Line thinking. For example, "I understand why you feel that way about the Patient Satisfaction Scores. I would probably think that way, too, if I were in your shoes. But bear with me a minute. Let me share a different perspective."

Step 3: Create a Compelling Case for the New Narrative

As we have said repeatedly in this book, you can't command or force people to change and expect it to result in positive, lasting change. People need the opportunity to choose for themselves whether they will change. You must make a compelling case for change that convinces them that it's in their best interest and is the best way to get the needed results. Of course, you need to also model the change yourself. What you're doing is creating a new, more powerful narrative to replace the old one. For example, "Our survey shows that understaffing does not fully explain our slow progress, but let's set that aside for the moment. I'd like to tell you about St. Mary's Hospital in Detroit. It gets better scores than we do with a much lower nurse-to-patient ratio. One of their administrators recently shared with us an amazing story about getting more with less."

Step 4: Invite Your People to Help Define the New Narrative

Rather than impose a new narrative on the organization, encourage your people to tell you the beliefs that should help shape a new narrative. Most of us like to tell and listen to good stories. For example, "You can see why I love that story about St. Mary's. I wonder if you've seen anything like that happen here in the past two years. We're looking for examples that illustrate this new way of working."

When you hear a good story that supports the change initiative, repeat it frequently and ask your people to retell it until it becomes part of the new narrative. It will likely take many stories and many weeks or months, but a new narrative will emerge, and that new narrative will do more to promote a desired culture change than all the memos and mandates in the world.

3. Weave Accountability into the Culture

What happens if past experiences tell people that someone's head will roll whenever a leader says, "Who's accountable for this mistake?" Of course, the resulting belief bias will prompt all the usual actions: excuse making, finger-pointing, and expressions of victimization. This always leads to disappointing outcomes. If you want people to accept accountability as a positive, propelling force for getting results, say it before, not after, the fact. "Who's accountable for achieving this result?" When you say it before the fact, people will understand that the power to get results lies in their own hands. They will strive, voluntarily, for a satisfying outcome.

With every one of our clients we apply the Sixteen Best Practices associated with the Steps to Accountability. There are four best practices for each of the Steps to Accountability, enabling you to take inventory of the opportunities you have to weave greater accountability into the culture of your team or organization. Take a moment and give your organization or team a grade of A, B, C, D, or F for each best practice. Select your grade based on the extent to which the respective best practice is demonstrated and embedded in your team or organization. Answer the questions that are listed beneath each of the Sixteen Best Practices to help you select the most appropriate and accurate grade.

Sixteen Best Practices

SEE IT

Obtaining the Perspectives of Others: _____
(Grade)

- How well do we gather others' perspectives?

- Do we apply this to every level in our organization, as well as to people outside our organization, such as suppliers, customers, and even competitors?

Communicating Openly and Candidly: _____
(Grade)

- Do we cover every important topic—especially the ones that make us feel uncomfortable—during a meeting rather than in the hallway after the meeting?

- Do we encourage honest discussion and debate?

Asking for and Offering Feedback: _____ (Grade)

- Do we make feedback a daily habit?

- Do we give and receive feedback in a positive, appreciative way?

Hearing the Hard Things: _____ (Grade)

- Do we welcome the truth about a situation without fear of defeat or retribution?

- Do we acknowledge the realities that are getting in the way of achieving Key Results?

OWN IT

Demonstrating Personal Investment: _____ (Grade)

- Do we keep people involved in what's happening throughout our organization, or do we allow people to say, "It's not my job"?

- Do we seek agreement that getting Key Results is everyone's job?

Learning from Both Success and Failure: _____ (Grade)

- Do we encourage people to risk failure and learn from mistakes and setbacks?

- Do we learn from our successes and reward people accordingly?

Aligning Work with the Key Results: _____ (Grade)

- Does everyone see how their work connects to Key Results?

- Do people align their work priorities with those Key Results?

Acting on Feedback: _____ (Grade)

- Do we communicate our willingness to act on the feedback we receive?

- Do we expect others to act on the feedback we give?

SOLVE IT

Asking Constantly "What Else Can I Do?": _____ (Grade)

- Do we stress "else" (different) rather than "more"?

- Do we emphasize the need for creative problem solving and innovation?

Collaborating across Functional Boundaries: _____ (Grade)

- Do we remove obstructing silos?

- Do we foster cross-functional communication and collaboration?

Conquering Obstacles: _____ (Grade)

- Do we look for ways over or around roadblocks to success?

- Do we welcome bold new ideas for solving problems?

Taking the Necessary Risks: _____ (Grade)

- Do we take risks in the face of potential failure?

- Do we encourage and reward calculated risk taking?

DO IT

Doing the Things I Say I'll Do: _____ (Grade)

- Are people doing what they say they'll do?

- Do we leave meetings with action lists detailing who will do what by when?

- Do we follow up on those commitments?

Staying Above the Line by Not Blaming Others: _____ (Grade)

- Do we discourage excuse making and blaming others?

- Do we respectfully call people out for slipping Below the Line?

Identifying the "Who" in "Who Will Do What by When?": _____ (Grade)

- Do we define roles before and during a meeting?

- Do people accept new roles when necessary?

Creating and Sustaining an Environment of Trust: _____ (Grade)

- Do we interact with others in a spirit of humility, honesty, and respect?

- Do we let people know we expect the same from them?

Adopting and perfecting the Sixteen Best Practices will help you create a Culture of Accountability, the best gift you will ever give your organization. It's worth repeating: Either you manage your culture, or it will manage you.

Getting Accountability
Right: Manage Your Culture

1. A large casual dining restaurant establishment placed a year-long moratorium on any new "IT Projects" until existing stability levels on their current technology platforms reached certain levels. The CEO sent a clear message that the company's culture stresses executing on current priorities without allowing other distractions to compromise successful implementation.

2. The leadership team of a credit union in the southeastern United States took turns working shifts as bank tellers within their branches. The team's intent was to better understand their guest experience firsthand. This experience exemplified a Culture of Accountability and was visible to every employee in the organization.

3. We worked with the chief operating officer of a major medical device company who consistently began his executive leadership meeting by asking, "What feedback did you receive this week that you found valuable and what are you doing to act on it?" His consistency in asking this question reinforced the belief that he was entirely committed to developing leaders who could effectively and consistently See It. He developed a feedback-rich environment and created a Culture of Accountability wherein results flourished.

4. The head of pharmaceutical sales, responsible for an $8 billion per year drug, brought his leadership team together once per quarter. While together they graded themselves on the Sixteen

Best Practices under See It, Own It, Solve It, and Do It. They soon found that this exercise facilitated the most honest and candid conversations about their business. Those conversations kept the business growing in spite of the dire predictions made by experts following the entrance of generics in their space.

Conclusion

ACCOUNTABILITY AS "THE WAY WE DO THINGS AROUND HERE"

In the Introduction we gave you a succinct summary of *The Oz Principle* that can help you make Accountability the "Way We Do Things Around Here," no matter who you're with or where you are.

> Only when you assume full accountability for your thoughts, feelings, actions, and results can you direct your own destiny; otherwise someone or something else will.

We hope you have enjoyed experiencing the impact that implementing *The Oz Principle* can have on you, your team, and your organization. We also encourage you to use *Propeller*, the book, and *Propeller*, the app, to accelerate and sustain the needed change in yourself and the people you work with in order to achieve the results you want, year after year.

Finally, in the spirit of "what else can we do?," we'd like to leave you with a final story that personifies the positive, propelling power of *The Oz Principle.*

Mike Stenson, SVP of sales for a specialty pharmaceutical company, discovered a serious problem in his St. Louis territory. Performance had sagged to the bottom of a deep, dark pit. When Mike called the territory's manager, "Joe," to discuss the situation, he heard a litany of explanations about why the territory was underperforming.

"I'll never forget that conversation," Mike recalls. "Joe wasted no time launching into a list of all the reasons he couldn't sell our products in the St. Louis–based territory." For thirty minutes, he languished Below the Line and blamed the marketing department, the lack of leadership from the C-suite to his regional manager, the researchers who had failed to develop superior products, and even the weather. "It's been the rainiest, coldest spring on record." Mike smiled to himself, thinking, *I guess Joe would be a sales superstar, if he only had. . . .*

Perhaps St. Louis really was a black hole. Maybe his company should concentrate its efforts elsewhere. Then Mike pulled back the curtain and saw the truth. Joe had gotten hopelessly sucked into adopting an alluring, albeit false, narrative. "It's an impossible situation. It's not my fault. My territory is remarkably infertile. If corporate would only give me more resources. They aren't being clear enough with the strategy." By the end of the call Mike realized that he would have to find someone else to tackle the St. Louis territory.

After advising Joe that he should look for a job better suited to his talents, he replaced him with a seasoned sales professional named Sandy Crouch. Sandy brought an impressive track record to her new job. She had sold everything from industrial appliances to ball bearings in the St. Louis area. Impressed by her can-do attitude and her eagerness to show her stuff in the troubled territory, Mike gave her six months to turn it around.

Initial conversations Sandy conducted with sales prospects revealed that people did not put much faith in the company's products, largely due to a lack of solid information about them. The company's products suffered from such low brand awareness that Sandy decided she would need to start from scratch, pretending she was selling products for a brand-new start-up.

Fast-forward six months. Mike began to see a dramatic uptick in sales orders from St. Louis. At first Sandy reported a trickle of new business, a sale or two a week, but before long the trickle became a stream, and the stream became a flood. Just nine months into Sandy's stewardship, the territory was racking up record numbers, and a year later it had surpassed every other territory in the company in new revenue. No one applauded more heartily than Mike when Sandy strode to the podium at the company's annual Circle of Excellence Awards night to accept a Crystal Goblet Award for her achievements.

After the banquet Sandy explained the turnaround. "I knew that I was taking over a pretty rough territory, and the first few months were a nightmare. I couldn't get my foot in any door. But I decided to keep pounding away until I landed one new customer. I lay awake at night wondering what more I could do to convince just *one* customer to give our products a try. I got more info from R&D and marketing, I thoroughly researched the competition, and I asked you and our other reps for advice so many times, you probably thought I was a pest. But I landed that first sale, and I jumped on it. They gave our products rave reviews that impressed the heck out of other customers. After I closed a second sale, then a third, the good word spread like wildfire."

The moral of the Sandy Crouch story? The moral of this entire book? Stop complaining and blaming others for your problems and take accountability for the results you need. To this day Mike cites Sandy as a prime example of the incredible power of accountability. "Sandy *saw* the problem, *owned* the problem, figured out how to *solve* it, then went out and *did* it. See It, Own It, Solve It, Do It: That's how you harness the incredible power of accountability."

Like many people working in today's turbulent business environment, you may share the same feelings of anxiety and helplessness that beset Dorothy, the Scarecrow, the Lion, and the Tin Man on their journey. In the end, however, those feelings disappeared when the truth finally dawned on them that only they could get the results they desired. Such a realization replaces pessimism with optimism, finger-pointing with embracing of responsibility, and victimization with powerful and proactive engagement focused on delivering desired results.

A lack of accountability can creep into any organization. It may first come unannounced as a reasonable explanation; then it may escalate into a more aggressive blame-oriented accusation; and then, over time, it simply becomes "the way we do things around here." That narrative in an organization can take over and inevitably lead to failure. Success comes from applying a more proactive version of accountability. A version focused on *taking* accountability for better results. Not being held accountable after the fact. Make *taking accountability* the way we do things around here and see how your results change.

Take accountability for the results you need. Apply *The Oz Principle*. Stay Above the Line to See It, Own It, Solve It, and Do It. Propel yourself, your team, and your organization to a brighter and better future.

Acknowledgments

We acknowledge all of the people we have encountered in our client organizations around the world who have helped shape our deeper understanding of the principles laid out in this book. We deeply appreciate all of the enthusiastic readers who spread the word about the first two editions of *The Oz Principle,* upon which this book is based. They have carried the message of accountability to many of the most successful organizations in the world.

We particularly thank our parents, spouses, children, clients, and our fellow workers at Partners In Leadership.

We also feel indebted to all of the people who reviewed and offered feedback on the manuscript: Brent Barton, Kent Robinson, Lisa Miller, Tracy Skousen, Marcus Nicolls, Lawrence Corbridge, Brad Starr, and Ryan Millar. We also wish to thank our editors, Vivian Roberson, Olivia Peluso, Nina Rodríguez-Marty and the team at Penguin Random House, for their patient guidance and thoughtful editing. Our publisher, Adrian Zackheim, has provided strong

ACKNOWLEDGMENTS

encouragement and support for almost three decades. Thank you, Adrian. We too are grateful for the unflagging commitment of our collaborator and agent Michael Snell.

Finally, we thank you, dear reader, for joining us on the journey to results through accountability. May it change your life as much as it has ours.

Index

INDEX

INDEX

Meet  the App

Align your team.
Inspire ownership.
Get results.

The *Propeller* app improves team performance by inspiring higher levels of personal engagement, ownership, and accountability for results. Intuitive features enable you to define and effectively communicate the team's top-priority outcomes, coach team members to take ownership of the right things, and hand everyone a suite of practical, everyday tools rooted in "See It, Own It, Solve It, Do It" that inspire positive accountability and impact results.

The *Propeller* app, which can be used by teams of any size on the phone, tablet, and computer, engages team members in four time-tested and value-added areas of collaboration and learning.

 Key Results—Aligning around the top-priority outcomes the team must work together to deliver.

 Feedback—Coaching each other in the moment, fostering "can do" mind-sets, and discovering areas of personal growth that most impact team success.

 Solve It—Collaborating to overcome obstacles and accelerate progress on Key Results.

 Wisdom—Applying principles and tools daily to create a Culture of Accountability for delivering needed results.

◉ Key Results

Get everyone aligned and focused, and keep them there—quickly, effectively.

Ensuring clarity and alignment on shared outcomes is foundational to effective leadership, yet even skilled and experienced leaders struggle to define and communicate the top-priority outcomes—the Key Results—they need people to take accountability to deliver. The challenge is only made worse by ever-increasing market disruption, the accelerating speed of change, the rise of remote work, the epidemic of disengagement afflicting workforces at home and abroad, and siloed communication that lets employees' concerns and questions go unheard and unanswered and allows confusion to fester where clarity is needed.

Propeller's Key Results tool enables leaders to cut through the noise and confusion to clearly define and effectively communicate Key Results and get team members aligned in their commitment to achieve them. How can an app do that?

Defining and Communicating Key Results

Propeller provides guidance and tools enabling leaders in any kind or size of team to craft Key Results that are meaningful, measurable, and memorable—results that make sense, foster a sense of purpose, and inspire commitment.

When leaders add a Key Result in *Propeller*, team members receive email and push notifications, and the app places these core priorities at everyone's fingertips on a dedicated, interactive Key Results page. The team also sees the current status of each result—on track, at risk, or off track—as set by the leader.

Alongside the Key Results, *Propeller* enables leaders to send video messages to their team to foster understanding and buy-in, celebrate wins, and share important news.

Creating and Maintaining Alignment

Within each Key Result, leaders and team members tap into four alignment-building channels of communication.

- **Updates**—Where leaders communicate progress toward the Key Result to their team.

- **Q&A**—Where team members openly stream comments and questions about the result, and leaders provide answers in real time to ensure understanding and foster common purpose.

- **My Impact**—Where leaders and team members collaborate to describe how everyone personally contributes to the result. As My Impact statements stream in, each person's tie to the Key Results becomes transparent team-wide.

- **Ownership**—Where team members confidentially set their level of ownership and the team's overall level of ownership is objectively assessed—providing affirmation when buy-in is high as well as an early warning should a decline in ownership put a Key Result at risk.

 # Feedback

Give and receive feedback that propels your team forward.

Propeller's Feedback tool enables teams to rapidly increase feedback that accelerates personal growth and expands the team's ability to achieve desired results. In *Propeller*, leaders and team members leverage feedback in four ways:

- **Endorse**—Where team members tap through an accountability card deck and recognize peers when demonstrating mind-sets and behaviors that deliver results.

- **Exchange**—Where team members seek and offer feedback through a simple workflow that ties appreciative and constructive communication to shared values and objectives.

- **Suggest**—Where team members share awesome ideas that accelerate progress toward Key Results.

- **My Feedback**—Where team members track and continue their feedback exchanges over time.

 Solve It

Crowdsource your team intelligence to accelerate idea generation and problem solving.

Propeller's Solve It tool enables leaders and team members to identify and crowdsource solutions to problems as they arise. Within Solve It, leaders and team members can:

- Quickly share any team-wide issues, problems, or obstacles that are slowing progress toward Key Results.

- Maximize team involvement to find and rank the best solutions.

- Follow problems of interest and collaborate on solutions to accelerate progress.

- Sort suggested solutions according to personal and team preferences.

- Share adopted solutions to keep the team informed and aligned.

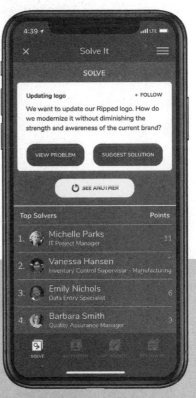

Well Played

Propeller appeals to the natural desire for achievement and recognition by awarding points for solving problems, exchanging feedback, and receiving endorsements. A leaderboard in Solve It also profiles the ten "top solvers" on the team.

 # Wisdom

Grow your team's understanding of culture, accountability, and results.

Within *Propeller's* Wisdom tool, the principles and models that create greater accountability for results are just a tap away for use in meetings, one-on-ones, and daily work. Micro-lessons accompany each principle and model, providing brief explanations, how-tos, and quick-links to *Propeller* features that translate concepts to practice.

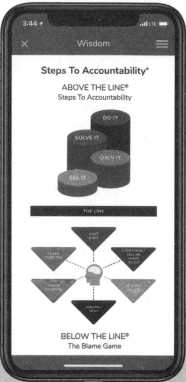

propeller™

We chose the title *Propeller* for both the book and the app because it captures in one word what each aims to create: **accelerated movement in a needed direction**. No matter how daunting the obstacles you face, *Propeller*, the book, will deepen your resolve to take accountability for your results—past, present, and future. *Propeller*, the app, will help embed the lessons of the book into practice to get your team and organization aligned and focused on what matters most. Visit **www.propellerapp.com** for more.